*Aquinas Scripture Series Vol. 1*

# COMMENTARY
## on SAINT PAUL'S
## EPISTLE to the
## GALATIANS

*by St. Thomas Aquinas*

Translated by F. R. Larcher, O.P.
Introduction by Richard T. A. Murphy, O.P.

Magi Books, Inc.

33 Buckingham Dr.                    Albany, N. Y. 12208

Library of Congress Catalog Card Number: 66–19306

FOR THE MOST PART THE TEXTS OF THE BIBLE ARE THOSE
AS TRANSLATED IN THE VERSION PUBLISHED BY C T S, 39
ECCLESTON SQUARE, LONDON, S.W. I, ENGLAND.

MANUFACTURED IN THE UNITED STATES OF AMERICA
PRINTED BY THE HAMILTON PRINTING CO.
NIHIL OBSTAT: J. S. CONSIDINE, O.P., J. W. CURRAN, O.P.
IMPRIMI POTEST: GILBERT J. GRAHAM, O.P. IMPRIMATUR:
MOST REV. LOUIS J. REICHER, D.D., BISHOP OF AUSTIN, 20
DECEMBER 1965.

Each volume in the *Aquinas Scripture Series* will
contain an illustration from the rare *Vita D. Thomae
Aquinatis.* Othonis Vaeni ingenio et manu delineata.
Antverpiae Sumptibus Othonis Vaeni, 1610.

The present portrait by Boel is not intended as an
historical likeness.

# EFFIGIES D. THOMÆ AQVINATIS:

*Quem Ecclesia Doctorem, scholæ magistrum, hæretici flagellum habuere: quemᵠ Pius Papa V. quintum Ecclesiæ Doctorem nominare solebat. Hunc Italia nascentem vidit, sanguinis nobilitas celebrauit. Auus eius fuit Comes Sommacolensis, qui Frederici II. Imp. sorore ducta Landulphum progenuit, cui Theodora Comitis Theanensis filia sanctum Thomam peperit.*

C. Boel

# Contents

# Introduction

It is a pleasure to write this introduction to Father Richard Larcher's smooth, workmanlike translation of St. Thomas Aquinas' commentary, appearing now for the first time in English, on St. Paul's famous letter to the Galatians.

A word about this letter. More than any other of Paul's writings, it tells us much about his life, and provides many details from that difficult period when the early Church was establishing her own true identity apart from the matrix of Judaism. The Old Testament mold was not to be broken easily, and St. Paul, who did so much to hasten the process, paid a heavy price for his contribution to it. His reputation and authority were challenged, his motives and teaching impugned, and his good name vilified; Galatians tells us all this. The Churches Paul had founded in that northern territory (in the center of what is now known as Turkey) were threatened by a large scale apostasy and Christianity was in imminent danger of being there transformed into a Jewish sect. The severity of the crisis explains the explosive tone of Paul's letter. Galatians is a burning, emotion-filled manifesto. Hurrying through his customary salutation, Paul plunges headlong into a vehement defense of his authority to teach in Christ's name, describes his relationship with Peter and the Apostles, restates his "gospel" (1–2). He urgently recalls to his readers the supreme importance of Christ's redemptive death (3); man is not justified by the Law, but by faith. The true Christian is one bound to Christ not by practices and observances such as circumcision and Sabbath observance, but by faith and baptism. In other words, the Christian is a *free* man (4). Having made this point, Paul concludes his letter with practical exhortations: the Galatians must beware of enslavement, must use their new liberty in a responsible manner, and employ their time in an untiring pursuit of good works (5–6).

Notwithstanding the bellicose tone of his letter, Paul's affection for these fickle Galatian converts is unmistakeable. Behind his complaints, his worries, anger, urgent appeals, one perceives a Paul who is warm and friendly, a true Apostle.

A date in the neighborhood of 56–57 A.D. may be assigned to Galatians. Paul will write another more restrained and formal letter, along the same lines, to the Romans. As this is dated to 57 A.D., the two letters resemble each other strongly, and are mutually complementary.

❋   ❋   ❋

Throughout his entire teaching career, St. Thomas was, as befitted a *Master of the Sacred Page,* constantly preoccupied with the Bible. (Strange though it may seem to us now, the Bible, not the *Summa,* was the common textbook for all.) It is however impossible to establish with certainty the exact chronology of his biblical works. He is known to have commented on all of Paul's letters, once during the years 1259–65, and again from 1272–73, shortly before his death. Only the first section (Romans 1, 1 through 1 Corinthians 7, 9) of our printed editions of his commentaries on St. Paul are the work of St. Thomas himself; the remaining pages have been supplied from the notes taken down during his lectures by Peter of Tarentasia (for the section from 1 Corinthians 7, 10 to 9, 27) and by Reginald of Piperno (for all the rest). There is no reason to suppose that two such devoted disciples played their Master false; one merely regrets the circumstances which prevented Thomas from himself finishing his commentary on Paul.

St. Thomas' exegesis, naturally, reflects the condition of Bible studies of his day. Scientific study of the Scriptures, as we now know it, had not yet begun, nor indeed could it have even been thought of, until the invention of the printing press would stabilize the text; and two more centuries would elapse before that happy event occurred. The texts to which medieval scholars had access were quite uniformly poor; the most conscientious of monkish scribes sometimes nodded, and there was a flourishing over-supply of textual errors to mislead the reader. Thomas had at his disposal the Parisian Vulgate, not a particularly good text, although it featured the chapter divisions recently introduced into the Bible by Stephen Langton (1226). Also available to him was the *Correctorium* of the Bible made by the Dominicans of St. James' convent in Paris, under the direction of Hugh of St. Cher. In that busy convent there was also to be found a verbal concordance, by which one could speedily check on the various meanings given to a particular word in all parts of the Bible.

It seems certain that St. Thomas shared in the prevailing ignorance of biblical languages (Hebrew and Greek). In the present condition of our knowledge it is not possible to ascertain whether he ever owned a Greek Bible, but as he had obtained Greek texts of Aristotle (which he persuaded William of Moerbeke to translate for him), it may be reasonably supposed that he also had a Greek Bible. In any case, the text he commented on was that of the Vulgate.

He had, perforce, to work without any of the assistance archeology offers the Bible student of our day. Biblical archeology is a young science, scarcely a century old, and yet it provides the modern scholar with an enormous amount of extra-biblical material (of a religious, cultural, legal, and political nature) which often sheds light on the meaning of the sacred text. Thomas did well with the materials he had at hand, devoting no less than 41 lectures to the Galatian letter. He evinces little interest in some of the questions which occupy so much of the modern scholar's time: the destination of the letter (was it to the churches in north or south Galatia?), the date of its composition (was it written before or after the Council of Jerusalem [49–50]?), the supposed contradictions between Acts and Galatians, and so on. But the answers now advanced for these complicated problems are far from conclusive, and in any case, answers to that type of question are of rather secondary importance. What is really important here is what Paul thought and taught. His letter is sacred and inspired—the Church assures us of this—and the text as it stands calls imperiously for interpretation and understanding. The present commentary, therefore, is important. In wrestling with St. Paul's teaching, our believing Thomas, the theologian *par excellence*, is in his proper element. Some may find his rigid procedure, his methodical analysis of the text, both galling and irksome; they should perhaps be warned in advance not to overlook St. Thomas' astounding familiarity with the entire Bible and his unflagging interest in the literal meaning of Paul's words. He makes many shrewd, penetrating remarks in these pages, and these alone are well worth the trouble of their discovery. The combination of the Apostle to the Gentiles and the Angel of the Schools is not one lightly to be dismissed.

❖   ❖   ❖

But *let this be enough by way of preface, for it is a foolish thing to make a long prologue, and to be short in the story itself* (2 Machabees 2, 33). From here on the Dumb Ox of Aquino will speak eloquently of Paul, and more eloquently still, of God.

*Aquinas Institute*
*School of Theology*          RICHARD T. A. MURPHY, O.P.
Dubuque, Iowa

# PROLOGUE

*The new coming on, you shall cast away the old.* (Lev. 26:10)

These words befit the present epistle in which the Apostle reproves the Galatians who had been so deceived by false teachers as to observe at once the rites of the Law and those of the Gospel. For this the Apostle rebukes them with the above words: *"The new coming on, you shall cast away the old."* In these words the Lord suggests a fourfold oldness.

First, the oldness of error concerning which Isaias states (26:3): "The old error is passed away." This is removed by the newness of the doctrine of Christ. "What is this new doctrine?" (Mk. 1:27).

The second oldness is that of figure, concerning which Hebrews (8:8) states: "Behold, the days shall come, saith the Lord; and I will perfect, unto the house of Israel and unto the house of Juda, a new testament not according to the testament which I made to their fathers." Here he shows first of all that the first testament is old and that it is made new by the newness of grace or of the reality of Christ's presence. "The Lord hath created a new thing upon the earth . . ." (Jer. 31:22).

The third is the oldness of guilt, concerning which Psalm (31:3) states: "Because I was silent" (not confessing my sins), "my bones grew old." And this is made new by the newness of justice. "So we may walk in newness of life" (Rom. 6:4).

The fourth is the oldness of punishment. "My skin he

1

hath made old" (Lam. 3:4). And this will be made new by the newness of glory, concerning which Isaias (66:22) states: "Behold I will create a new heaven and a new earth." "And he that sat on the throne said: Behold, I make all things new" (Apoc. 21:5).

# CHAPTER 1

## LECTURE 1

1 Paul, an apostle, not of men, neither by man, but by Jesus Christ and God the Father, who raised him from the dead,

2 And all the brethren who are with me, to the churches of Galatia:

3 Grace be to you, and peace from God the Father and from our Lord Jesus Christ,

4 Who gave himself for our sins, that he might deliver us from this present wicked world, according to the will of God and our Father;

5 To whom is glory for ever and ever. Amen.

The Apostle therefore writes the Galatians this epistle in which he shows that with the coming of the grace of the New Testament, the Old Testament should be cast out, so that with the fulfillment of the truth, the figure may be abandoned, and with the attainment of these two, namely, grace and truth, one may arrive at the truth of justice and glory. And these two are acquired, if, abandoning the observance of the "legalia" [i.e., the ceremonial precepts of the Old Law], we concentrate fervently on observing the Gospel of Christ.

The order of this epistle is fitting in that, after the two epistles to the Corinthians, in the first of which it is a question of the sacraments of the Church, and in the second, of the ministers of these sacraments, there should necessarily follow the epistle to the Galatians, treating of the termination of the sacraments of the Old Testament.

This epistle is divided into two parts: namely, into a greeting, and the setting forth of the epistle (v. 6): **I won-**

3

**der that you are so soon removed from him that called you
into the grace of Christ, unto another gospel.** In the greeting, however:

> First, the person who sends the greeting is mentioned;
> Secondly, the persons greeted are mentioned (v. 2):
> **To the Churches of Galatia;**
> Thirdly, the good he wishes them (v. 3).

As to the first, mention is made first of the person principally sending the greeting; and he is described by his name and his authority. By his name, indeed, when he says **Paul** which, because it means "humble," accords with his humility. Hence it is said in I Corinthians (15:9): "I am the least of the apostles, who am not worthy to be called an apostle." Furthermore, it accords with his office, because in another sense it means "the mouth of the trumpet," in which the office of preaching is specially signified. "Lift up thy voice like a trumpet and announce to my people their sins" (Is. 58:1). He is described by his authority, when he says, **an apostle.** Here two things are mentioned, namely, his authority and its source. Authority, because he says **apostle,** which is the same as "sent."

Now it should be noted that the Apostle in some epistles calls himself "servant," thereby showing a spirit of humility, as in the Epistle to the Romans; in others he calls himself "apostle," thereby showing his authority. The reason for this is that the Romans being proud, the Apostle, in order to induce them to humility, calls himself a servant as an example of humility. But to the Galatians, who were stupid and proud, he calls himself an apostle in order to break them down; hence he here sets forth his authority.

He describes the source of his authority when he says, **not of men, neither by man, but by Jesus Christ, and God the Father.**

> First, he removes what is, according to their opinion, the source;

Secondly, he presents the true source (v. 1): **but by Jesus Christ and God the Father.**

The source [of his authority] in their opinion was in keeping with the fact that the Galatians had been so deceived by false teachers as to believe that the Apostle did not enjoy the same authority as the other apostles, as having neither been taught by Christ nor lived with Him, but sent by them as their minister. He therefore removes this opinion when he says, **not of men, neither by man.** For some had been sent by the whole college of apostles and disciples; hence, to show that he had not been sent by them, he says, **not of men.** Others had been sent by some particular apostle, as Paul now and then sent Luke and Titus. Therefore, to show that he had not been sent in that manner, he says, **neither by man,** i.e., not by any apostle in particular, but by the Holy Spirit, Who says: "Separate me Saul and Barnabas, for the work whereunto I have taken them "(Ac. 13:2).

But because the true cause of the origin of this authority is Christ Jesus, he says, **but by Jesus Christ and God the Father.** Now the distinction expressed when he says, **by Jesus Christ *and* God the Father,** can be taken with respect to the person of the Father and the person of the Son; and then God the Father is one person and Jesus Christ another. For the Blessed Apostle Paul was sent to preach by both, and indeed, by the whole Trinity, because the works of the Trinity are inseparable. Yet no mention is made of the person of the Holy Spirit, because, since there is a union and joining of two, by mentioning two persons, namely, Father and Son, the Holy Spirit too is understood. Or, the aforesaid distinction can be taken with respect to the assumed nature, i.e., the human, because according to the divine nature there is not a distinction between God the Father and Jesus Christ. In this sense, then, Paul was sent by God the Father as by the chief sender, and by Jesus Christ as by a minister. "For I say that Christ Jesus was minister of the circumcision" (Rom. 15:8).

But because the Galatians belittled the Apostle for having neither lived with Christ, as did the others, nor been sent by Him, he extols himself on this very point, because they had been sent by Christ yet living in mortal flesh, whereas he had been sent by Christ now glorified. This is why he says, **who,** namely, God the Father, **raised him,** namely, Jesus Christ as man, **from the dead.** As though to say: I am an apostle **not of men,** i.e., not by the college of apostles, **neither by man,** namely, Christ living in mortal flesh, but I am an apostle through Christ now risen and glorified. "Christ rising again from the dead, dieth now no more" (Rom. 6:9). And because the present life is signified by the left side and the future life by the right, inasmuch as the latter is heavenly and spiritual, and the former temporal, Peter, who was called while Christ was yet in mortal flesh, appears in papal bulls on the left side, but Paul, who was called by Christ now glorified, is set on the right side.

Then when he says, **and all the brethren who are with me,** he refers to the persons who join with him in sending the greeting. These he describes in terms of sweet familiarity, because they **are with me,** namely, for consolation and help. "A brother that is helped by his brother is like a strong city" (Prov. 18:19). "Behold how good and how pleasant it is for brethren to dwell together in unity" (Ps. 132:1). And in terms of inseparable charity, when he says, **brethren.** "By this shall all men know that you are my disciples, if you have love one for another" (Jn. 13:35). And universality, when he says, **all.** He adds this because they might be so deceived as not to respect the words of Paul. Hence he says, **all who are with me,** to show them as witnesses to his truthfulness and make it easy for them to understand that they are wrong, when they are rebuked by everyone else. "To him who is such a one, this rebuke is sufficient which is given by many" (2 Cor. 2:6).

He mentions the persons greeted when he says, **to the**

**churches of Galatia.** Here it should be noted that, as is mentioned in a Gloss, Brennus, leader of the Senones, once gathered an army, and having entered Italy through which he passed, came into Greece before the time of Alexander the Great. There some of the invaders remained in a certain district of Greece and intermarried with the Greeks. For this reason that province came to be called "Gallic Greece" and the inhabitants "Galatians," as it were, "white." But whereas the Greeks are natively intelligent, those Galatians were stupid and inconstant and slow to understand, as the indocile Gauls from whom they descended. This is why he later says, **O senseless Galatians, who hath bewitched you that you should not obey the truth?** (3:1). To these people, therefore, he writes this epistle, and they are the ones greeted.

Then when he says, **grace be to you and peace,** he mentions the good things he wishes them.

First, he mentions the goods he wishes;
Secondly, the author of these goods (v. 3): **from God the Father and our Lord.**

The goods he wishes them are twofold, but in them are included all spiritual goods. The first is **grace,** which is the beginning of the spiritual life, and to it is ascribed in a Gloss the remission of sins, which is first in the spiritual life. For no one can be in the true spiritual life, unless he first dies to sin. The second is **peace,** which is the settling down of the mind in its end, and which in a Gloss is said to be reconciliation with God. Thus in wishing them the beginning and the end of all spiritual goods, the Apostle includes, as it were, between the two extremes, the wish that every good come to them. "The Lord will give grace and glory" (Ps. 83:12). "The grace of Our Lord Jesus Christ and the charity of God and the communication of the Holy Spirit be with you all" (2 Cor. 13:13).

The author of these goods is God the Father, and so he says, **from God the Father.** Here are mentioned

First, the cause of the goods;
Secondly, the manner of causing (v. 4);
Thirdly, thanksgiving for these goods (v. 5).

The cause and source of good is God the Father as originator, precisely as God, and the entire Trinity, the God of
all through creation. "But Thou, O Father, governest it"
(Wis. 14:3). Hence he says, **from God the Father.** Again,
the originator is the Lord Jesus Christ as minister; and this
insofar as He is man. "For I say that Jesus Christ was a
minister" (Rom. 15:8). But that grace comes to us through
Christ is plain from John (1:17): "Grace and truth came by
Jesus Christ." "Being justified freely by His grace" (Rom.
3:24). Peace, too, comes to us through Him. "My peace I
give unto you" (Jn. 14:27).

The manner in which these goods are caused is also mentioned when he says, **who gave himself for our sins.** Here
is mentioned, first of all, the efficient cause, which is the
death of Christ. Referring to this, he says **who gave himself
for our sins.** As if to say: Christ is the author of grace and
peace, because He gave Himself to death and endured the
cross. Hence the very death of Christ is the efficient cause
of grace: "You have been justified freely by his grace" (Rom.
3:24); "Making peace as to the things that are in heaven"
(Col. 1:20). And he says, first of all, **who gave himself,** i.e.,
offered Himself voluntarily. "Christ also hath loved us and
hath delivered Himself for us" (Eph. 5:2); "That He might
taste death for all" (Heb. 2:9); "Who gave Himself for us"
(Tit. 2:14). From this, the Apostle plainly is arguing against
them that if the death of Christ is the sufficient cause of
our salvation, and if grace is conferred in the sacraments
of the New Testament, which have their efficacy from the
passion of Christ, then it is superflous to observe, along with
the New Testament, the rituals of the Old Law in which
grace is not conferred nor salvation acquired, because the
Law has led no one to perfection, as is had in Hebrews
(7:19).

Secondly, the end and utility of those goods is mentioned

—in other words, the final cause. And it is twofold; one is that we be set free of past sins; and as to this he says, **for our sins,** namely, that past sins be removed and atoned for, which is the beginning of our salvation. "He loved us and washed us from our sins in his own blood" (Apoc. 1:5). The other end is that He might free us from the power of death; and as to this he says, **that he might deliver us from this present wicked world.** "He delivered us from the power of darkness" (Col. 1:13). Herein he mentions three things: namely, **to deliver us from the present,** and the **world,** and **wicked.** To deliver us from the **present** by drawing us to eternal things through desire and hope; **from the world,** i.e., from being conformed to this world which allures us: "And be not conformed to this world" (Rom. 12:2); **wicked,** leading us back to the truth of justice. And it is called a wicked world, not because of its nature, for it was created good by God, but because of the evils perpetrated in it, as is said in Ephesians (5:16): "The days are evil." And "Jacob said: the days of my pilgrimage are a hundred and thirty years, few and evil" (Gen. 47:9).

Now although these things come to us through Christ, God the Father is not excluded. Hence there is mentioned in the third place, acceptance of the divine will. Therefore he says, **according to the will of God and our Father.** Of the Father by nature, I say, of Christ Who proceeds from eternity as the Word: "This day have I begotten Thee" (Ps. 2:7); "In the beginning was the Word, and the Word was with God, and the Word was God" (Jn. 1:1). Also of our Father by adoption: "He gave them power to be made the sons of God" (Jn. 1:12). In the first rendering, **God the Father** is taken for the sole person of the Father; in the second, for the whole Trinity. And because it is from God our Father, namely, from the whole Trinity, that all things come to us through Christ, therefore to it, i.e., to the whole Trinity, **glory** in itself, honor from others, be or is, **forever and ever,** i.e., always. **Amen.** This is a mark of corroboration.

You have therefore, in summary, in the above greeting,

the Apostle's authority by which he breaks their pride; the power of the grace by which he exhorts them to observe the Gospel; and the insufficiency of the ceremonies of the Law, in order to call them away from them.

# CHAPTER 1

## Lecture 2

6 I wonder that you are so soon removed from him that called you into the grace of Christ, unto another gospel;

7 Which is not another; only there are some that trouble you and would pervert the gospel of Christ.

8 But though we, or an angel from heaven, preach a gospel to you besides that which we have preached to you, let him be anathema.

9 As we said before, so now I say again: If any one preach to you a gospel, besides that which you have received, let him be anathema.

10 For do I now persuade men, or God? Or do I seek to please men? If I yet pleased men, I should not be the servant of Christ.

The greeting given, it is followed by the epistle message, in which the Apostle refutes their error; secondly, he admonishes them with a view to their correction (5:1): **Stand fast and be not held again under the yoke of bondage.** He refutes their error two ways: namely, on the authority of the Gospel teaching; and by reason, using the Old Testament (3:1): **O senseless Galatians, who hath bewitched you. . . ?**

He refutes their error by showing the authority of the Gospel teaching:

First, by showing their fickleness in lightly dismissing the Gospel teaching;

Secondly, by commending the authority of the Gospel

teaching, as he intimates that in view of the precious value of that which they so lightly regard, their error is seen to be so much the greater (v. 11).

Regarding the first he does two things:

First, he enlarges upon their guilt;
Secondly, he inflicts a punishment (v. 8).

Concerning the first, he enlarges upon the guilt both of the seduced and of those who seduced them (v. 7): **only there are some that trouble you.** As to the first he does three things:

First, he enlarges upon the guilt of those who were misled for their fickleness of mind. Hence he says, **I wonder.** As if to say: Although you are aware of the many good things already mentioned that come to you through Christ, and although I instructed you well, nevertheless you are **thus,** i.e., so far and so completely **removed** [transferred], that you seem already to have forgotten; **so soon,** i.e., in such a short time, are you **removed** [transferred]. With this word he alludes to their name, for Galatia means "transferred." As if to say: You are Galatians, because you are so quickly transferred. "He that is hasty to give credit is light of heart" (Ecclus. 19:4).

Secondly, he amplifies their guilt on the part of that which they have abandoned. For if reason withdraws and is removed from evil, it is worthy of praise and does well; but when it departs from the good, it is culpable. And this is how they were removed from good. So he says to them: Although it is amazing that you are so quickly and so far removed, there is additional reason for wonder, namely, because you have removed yourselves **from him,** i.e., from God, and from faith in Him **that called you into the grace of Christ,** i.e., into the sharing of the eternal good which we have through Christ: "Giving thanks to God who hath called you into his marvelous light" (1 Pet. 2:9). Again: "For it had been better for them not to have known the way of justice than, after they have known it, to turn back from that holy commandment which was delivered to them" (2 Pet. 2:21).

Thirdly, he amplifies their guilt on the part of that to which they have turned, because they have been turned not to good but to evil. Hence he says, **unto another gospel,** i.e., of the Old Law, which is a good message only insofar as it does announce some good things, namely, temporal and carnal: "If you be willing and will hearken to me, you shall eat the good things of the land" (Is. 1:19). Yet it is not completely perfect as is the Gospel, because it does not announce the perfect and loftiest goods, but small and slight ones. But the New Law is perfectly and in the full sense a Gospel, i.e., a good message, because it announces the greatest goods, namely, heavenly, spiritual and eternal. And although it is another gospel according to the tradition of the deceivers, yet according to my preaching it is not. For it is different in the promises, but not in the figure, because the same thing is contained in the Old Testament and in the New: in the Old, indeed, as in a figure, but in the New as in the express reality. Therefore it is another gospel if you consider the outward appearances; but as to the things that are contained and exist within, it is not another gospel.

Yet though it is not in itself another gospel, it can be another, if you consider the guilt of the others, i.e., of the deceivers. Hence in enlarging upon the guilt of the latter he says, **only there are some,** namely, the seducers, **that trouble you,** i.e., sully the purity of your understanding with which you were imbued with the truth of faith. Because although the same thing is contained, so far as the inward understanding is concerned, in the Old and New Testament, as has been said, yet if the Old is embraced after accepting the New, that is seen to show that the New is not perfect, and that the one is different from the other. Hence he says, **which is not another, only there are some that trouble you,** because those deceivers were compelling them to be circumcised after professing faith in the Gospel, showing thereby that circumcision is something different from Baptism and does something that Baptism cannot do, and for that reason they are troubling you. **I would that they were even cut off who trouble you** (5:12).

And they do indeed bring you trouble, because they **would pervert the gospel of Christ,** i.e., the truth of the Gospel teaching, into the figure of the Law—which is absurd and the greatest of troubles. For a thing ought to be converted into that to which it is ordained. But the New Testament and the Gospel of Christ are not ordained to the Old, but contrariwise, the Old Law is ordained to the New Law, as a figure to the truth. Consequently the figure ought to be converted into the truth, and the Old Law to the Gospel of Christ, not the truth into the figure, or the Gospel of Christ into the Old Law. This is plain from the way we ordinarily speak; for we do not say that a man resembles the image of a man, but contrariwise, that the image resembles the man: "They shall be turned to thee and thou shalt not be turned to them" (Jer. 15:19); "The new coming on, you shall cast away the old" (Lev. 26:10).

Then after enlarging upon their guilt, the inflicting of the penalty is set forth when he ways, **But though we, or an angel from heaven . . .** (v. 8). And with respect to this he does two things:

First, he promulgates the sentence;
Secondly, he gives a reason for the sentence (v. 10).

As to the first he does two things:

First, he presents authority for his sentence;
Secondly, he passes sentence (v. 9).

He shows that his authority for passing sentence is great on the ground that it would affect not only the perverters and seducers, who are subject to him, but also his own equals, as the other apostles, and even those above him, as the angels, were they guilty of this crime, namely, of turning the Gospel into the Old Law. Hence he says: Because the authority behind the sentence which we pass (which is excommunication) has efficacy, not only over those who are doing these things, then **though we,** namely, the apostles, **or an angel,** good or evil, coming **from heaven, preach a gospel besides that which we have preached, let him be anathema,** i.e., subject to this sentence that we pass.

To elucidate the foregoing, three things should be investigated. First, the meaning of this word, **anathema.** Apropos of this it should be noted that *anathema* is a Greek word composed of *ana,* which means *above,* and *thesis,* i.e., *a placing;* hence, *a placing above.* The word arose from an old custom. For the ancients, when they waged war, sometimes took from their enemies certain booty which they were unwilling to turn to their own use, but hung it in the temple or other public place of the city, as though to separate it from the common use of men. Everything so hung up, the Greeks called *anathema.* And from this arose the custom of declaring anathematized anything excluded from common use. Hence in Josue (6:17) it is said of Jericho and of everything in it, that Josue once anathematized it. Consequently, even in the Church the practice arose of declaring anathema those who are excluded from the common society of the Church and from partaking of the sacraments of the Church.

Secondly, we must look for an explanation of his statement, **though we, or an angel from heaven, preach a gospel to you besides that which we have preached to you, let him be anathema.** Here it should be noted that there are three kinds of teachings: the first is that of the philosophers who have arrived at a knowledge of their doctrine with their own reason guiding them. Another is that which has been delivered by angels, as the Old Law. For the Old Law was not issued by a human will but by angels in the hand of a mediator (Gal. 3:19). But the third teaching was given immediately by God Himself, as the teaching of the Gospel: "No man has seen God at any time; the only begotten Son

who is in the bosom of the Father, he hath declared him"
(Jn. 1:18); "In these days [He] hath spoken to us by his
Son" (Heb. 1:2); "Which, having begun to be declared by
the Lord, was confirmed unto us by them that heard him"
(Heb. 2:3).

Now, a teaching passed on by a man can be changed
and revoked by another man who knows better, as one philosopher refutes the sayings of another, or by an angel who
has a more penetrating knowledge of the truth. Even a
teaching handed down by one angel could be supplanted by
that of a higher angel or by God. But a teaching that comes
directly from God can be nullified neither by man nor angel.
Hence if a man or an angel were to state anything contrary
to what has been taught by God, such a statement would
not contradict God's teaching, so as to void or destroy it;
rather, God's teaching would be against him, because one
who speaks thus should be expelled and prevented from
sharing his teaching. Hence the Apostle says that the dignity
of the Gospel teaching, which has come directly from God,
is so great that if a man or even an angel preached another
Gospel besides that which he has preached among them,
he is anathemia, i.e., must be rejected and expelled.

Thirdly, we must solve the objections which arise on
this point. The first is that, since an equal has no authority
over his peers and much less over his superiors, it seems that
the Apostle has no power to excommunicate the apostles, who
are his peers, and less so, angels who are superior. "He that
is the lesser in the kingdom of heaven is greater than he"
(Matt. 11:11). Therefore the anathema is invalid. The answer to this is that the Apostle passed this sentence not on
his own authority, but on the authority of the Gospel teaching, of which he was the minister, and the authority of which
teaches that whoever says aught contrary to it must be expelled and cast out. "The word that I have spoken, the same
shall judge him in the last day" (Jn. 14:48).

A second question arises from the words, **a gospel be-**

sides that which we have preached to you. Therefore no one may teach or preach anything but what is written in the epistles and Gospels. But this is false, because it is said in I Thessalonians (3:10): "Praying that we may accomplish those things that are wanting to your faith." I answer that nothing is to be taught except what is contained, either implicitly or explicitly, in the Gospels and epistles and Sacred Scripture. For Sacred Scripture and the Gospels announce that Christ must be believed explicitly. Hence whatever is contained therein implicitly and fosters its teaching and faith in Christ can be preached and taught. Therefore, when he says, **besides that which you have received,** he means by adding something completely alien: "If any man shall add to these things, God shall add unto him the plagues written in this book" (Apoc. 22:18). And "Neither add anything," i.e., contrary or alien, "nor diminish" (Deut. 12:32).

Then when he says, **As we said before, so now I say it again: If any one preach to you a gospel, besides that which you have received, let him be anathema,** he pronounces his sentence on the evil person and says: As I have said of angels and apostles, so I say of the seducers. If any seducer **shall preach a gospel besides that which you have received from me, let him be anathema,** i.e., excommunicated. And this is the sentence he passes.

Now it may be asked whether all heretics are thereby excommunicated. And it seems not, because it is said: "A man that is a heretic, after the first and second admonition, avoid" (Tit. 3:10). I answer that a person might be called a heretic either because he errs solely from ignorance, and then he is not on that account excommunicated; or because he errs through obstinacy and tries to subvert others, and then he falls under the canon of the sentence passed. But whether he was then and there passing sentence on heretics by these words is open to question, since sentence was later passed against heretics in the Councils. Yet it can be said that per-

haps he was showing that they deserved to be excommunicated.

Then when he says, **For do I now persuade men, or
God?,** he gives the reason for his sentence.

> First, he gives the reason for his sentence;
> Secondly, he discloses here his purpose (v. 10): **Or do
> I seek to please men?**

For someone might say: Why do you excommunicate in
this manner? Perhaps some are your friends or men of some
authority. Therefore you ought not act in this way. But the
Apostle says in answer: Indeed, one should act in this way,
because the things I say now are not to gain the favor of
men but to please God, and this is what he means by **do I
now,** i.e., after my conversion, or in this epistle, **persuade
men,** i.e., is it my intention to please men **or God?** As if to
say: The things I do, I do to please God alone: "We speak,
not as pleasing men, but God" (I Thess. 2:4); nor do we
speak on the authority of men, but of God. That I do not
seek to please men is plain from my intention and purpose.
For **I do not seek to please men,** i.e., it is not my intention
in converting men to please men alone, but for the honor
of God. And this is plain, because **if I yet** sought to **please
men,** as I formerly pleased them, **I should not be the servant
of Christ.** The reason is that the two are opposed. More precisely, if I were to please men for the sake of men without
referring it to God; for if I intend now and then to please
men so that I might draw them to God, I do not sin. But
if in the first way, I am not the servant of Christ: "For the
bed is straitened, so that one must fall out, and a short
covering cannot cover both" (Is. 28:20); "No man can serve
two masters. For either he will hate the one and love the
other; or he will sustain the one and despise the other" (Mt.
6:24); "They have been confounded that please men" (Ps.
52:6).

# CHAPTER 1

## LECTURE 3

11 For I give you to understand, brethren, that the gospel which was preached by me is not according to man.

12 For neither did I receive it of man; nor did I learn it but by the revelation of Jesus Christ.

13 For you have heard of my conversation in time past in the Jews' religion; how that, beyond measure, I persecuted the church of God and wasted it.

14 And I made progress in the Jews' religion above many of my equals in my own nation, being more abundantly zealous for the traditions of my fathers.

In the foregoing the Apostle rebuked the Galatians for their fickleness of mind in so quickly setting aside the Gospel teaching; now he shows the dignity of the Gospel teaching. And concerning this he does two things:

> First, he commends the authority of the Gospel teaching according to itself;
> Secondly, on the part both of the other apostles and himself (2:1): **Then, after fourteen years, I went up again to Jerusalem with Barnabas.**

The first part is further divided into two others, because

First, he presents his intention;
Secondly, he manifests his purpose (v. 13).

Regarding the first he does two things:

First, he proposes what he intends;
Secondly, he proves what he proposes (v. 12).

Intending, therefore, to commend the truth of the Gospel teaching, he says, **For I give you to understand,**

**brethren . . .** As if to say: So certain am I of the Gospel's authority, that I would disbelieve not only men but even angels saying the contrary; so that if they were contrary, I would say anathema to them. And I have this certainty, because one must believe God rather than men or angels. Therefore, since I have this Gospel from God, I should and do have the greatest of certainty. Hence he says, **For I give you to understand, brethren, that the gospel which was preached by me** to you and to the other Churches is **not according to man,** i.e., not according to human nature out of tune with the divine rule or divine revelation. In this sense, **according to man** implies something evil: "For whereas there is among you envying and contention, are you not carnal, and walk according to man?" (1 Cor. 3:3). And this is the sense the Apostle takes here; hence he says, **not according to man** teaching me or sending me. As if to say: Not at all can this Gospel be had from men but from God.

That is why he adds, **For neither did I receive it of man; nor did I learn it but by the revelation of Jesus Christ,** whereby he precludes two ways of receiving. First, that he did not receive from man the authority to preach. As to this he says, **nor of man,** i.e., purely man, **did I receive it,** i.e., the authority to preach the Gospel, but of Christ: "And how shall they preach unless they be sent?" (Rom. 10:15); "I have given thee for a light of the Gentiles, for a covenant of the people" (Is. 42:6); "This man is to me a vessel of election, to carry my name before the Gentiles and kings and the children of Israel" (Ac. 9:15). Secondly, that he did not receive the science of the Gospel from man. Hence he says, **nor did I learn it,** namely, the Gospel, from mere man, **but by the revelation of Jesus Christ,** i.e., by Jesus Christ showing everything clearly. "But to us, God hath revealed them" (1 Cor. 2:10); "The Lord hath opened my ear, and I do not resist" (Is. 50:5), and "The Lord has given me a learned tongue, that I should know how to uphold by word him that is weary" (Is. 50:4). Now this revelation was made to the Apostle when he was rapt into paradise, where "he heard secret words which it is not granted to man to utter" (2 Cor. 12:4).

Then when he says, **For you have heard of my conversation in time past,** he shows that he did not receive the Gospel from men, either before his conversion or after his conversion to Christ (v. 15). That he did not receive it from man before his conversion he shows both by the hatred he bore toward the faith of Christ and toward Christians, and by the zeal he had for Judaism: **And I made progress in the Jews' religion above many of my equals in my own nation** (v. 14).

He says therefore: I say that I did not receive it of man, and this is true of the time before my conversion. This, indeed, is obvious from my actions at that time and from the hatred I bore toward the faith. For you yourselves **have heard**—"But they had heard only: He who persecuted us in times past doth now preach the faith which once he impugned" (v. 23)—**of my conversation in time past,** when I was an unbeliever, **in the Jews' religion,** when I lived as a Jew. And he says, **my,** because the evil we do is from ourselves, but from God is whatever good we do: "Destruction is thy own, O Israel: thy help is only in me" (Os. 13:9).

This you have heard, **how that, beyond measure,** i.e., more than others, because he bestirred not only himself to this but rulers as well. For others, when they persecuted, were possibly led to it by the rulers, but he urged even them: "Saul, as yet breathing out threatenings and slaughter against the disciples of the Lord, went to the high priest" (Ac. 9:1). Also because he did this not only in Jerusalem but in the entire region. Hence "he received letters to Damascus, that if he found any men and women of this way, he might bring them bound to Jerusalem." Therefore what is said in Genesis (49:27): "Benjamin a ravenous wolf, in the morning shall eat the prey, and in the evening shall divide the spoil," can be understood as applying to him.

**I persecuted the church of God,** i.e., by hunting down Christians and discomfiting them: "I am not worthy to be called an apostle, because I persecuted the church of God" (1 Cor. 15:9); **and I wasted it,** not indeed spiritually, because I was unable to turn the hearts of the faithful from their faith, but physically by inflicting bodily punishment on them and casting them into prison: "Is not this he who persecuted in Jerusalem those that called upon this name?" (Ac. 9:21); "Often have they fought against me" (Ps. 128:1).

It is plain, therefore, from the hatred he bore toward the faith of Christ before his conversion, that he did not receive the Gospel from man.

It is plain also from the love and burning zeal he had for Judaism, as to outward progress. Hence he says, **And I made progress in the Jews' religion above many of my equals in my own nation:** wherein he mentions three things that indicate how great was his progress. For he progressed not above a few but **above many,** not above old men incapable of progress in learning, but **my equals,** i.e., young men who were intelligent and capable of progress: "It is good for a man, when he has borne the yoke from his youth" (Lam. 3:27). Furthermore, not above equals who were foreigners and ignorant of the language, but equals **of my own nation,** i.e., Jews: "I am a Jew, brought up at the feet of Gamaliel, taught according to the truth of the law of the fathers, zealous for the law, as also all you are this day" (Ac. 22:3).

Finally, as to the inward zeal he had for the Law. Hence he says, **being more abundantly zealous,** not only for the Law, but **for the traditions of my fathers,** namely, those traditions which the Jews lawfully kept and "which the good fathers added," as is said in a Gloss. He calls these traditions his own because he treasured them as though they were his: "According to the Law, a Pharisee; according to zeal, persecuting the church of God" (Phil. 3:5).

But a question arises from the fact that the aforesaid Gloss says: "The good fathers added." For it seems that they were not good, because it is said in Deuteronomy (4:2): "You shall not add to the word I speak to you." Hence in adding traditions they acted against the command of God and so were not good. To this one may answer that this word of the Lord is taken to mean that you shall not add anything contrary or alien to the words which I shall speak. But to add certain things not contrary was lawful for them, namely, certain solemn days and the like, as was done in the time of Mordochai and of Judith, in memory of the blessings they received from God.

But against this is the rebuke addressed to them by our Lord, when He says: "You have made void the command of the Lord for the traditions of men" (Mt. 15:16). Hence those traditions were not lawful.—I answer that they are not rebuked for holding the traditions of men, but because for the sake of the traditions of men, they neglect the commands of God.

# CHAPTER 1

## LECTURE 4

15 But when it pleased him who separated me from my mother's womb and called me by his grace
16 To reveal his Son in me, that I might preach him among the Gentiles; immediately I condescended not to flesh and blood.
17 Neither went I to Jerusalem, to the apostles who were before me; but I went into Arabia, and again I returned to Damascus.

After showing that he did not receive the Gospel from man before his conversion, the Apostle now proves that he did not receive it from man after his conversion. About this he does two things:

First, he shows that he did not receive the Gospel from man at the time of his conversion;

Secondly, nor after his conversion (v. 18).

Regarding the first he does two things:

First, he shows that he did not receive or learn the
    Gospel from the apostles;
Secondly, nor from any other believer (v. 17): **I went
    into Arabia, and again I returned to Damascus.**

As to the first he does three things:

First, he shows the efficient cause of his conversion;
Secondly, the end (v. 16);
Thirdly, the manner (v. 16): **immediately I condescended
    not to flesh and blood.**

In regard to the first point, he notes the twofold cause
of his conversion, namely, the good pleasure of God, which
is divine election, and the call of the one converting. Regarding the first he says, **when it pleased him,** namely, God: not
when I willed, but when it pleased Him, because "It is not
of him that willeth, nor of him that runneth, but of God
that sheweth mercy" (Rom. 9:16); "The Lord taketh pleasure
in them that fear him" (Ps. 146:11); "For it is God who
worketh in us, both to will and to accomplish, according to
his good will" (Phil. 2:13). **Who,** namely, God, **separated me,**
i.e., rebellious: "I am the least of the apostles, who am not
worthy to be called an apostle, because I persecuted the
church of God" (1 Cor. 15:9); "Saul, as yet breathing out
threatenings" (Ac. 9:1); and a persecutor: "Saul, Saul, why
persecutest thou me?" (Ac. 9:4); "Who before was a blas-
phemer" (1 Tim. 1:13). **Me,** and such a one, I say, **he separated from my mother's womb.** Or, literally: who made me
to be born from my mother's womb.

It is indeed true to say that God separates one from the
womb, even though it is a work of nature, which is, as it
were, an instrument of God, because even our own works
are attributed to God as to their principal author: "For thou
hast wrought all our works for us" (Is. 26:12), as any effect
is attributed to the principal agent; hence Job (10:11): "Thou
hast clothed me with skin and flesh." And he was separated

from this womb to be justified, for the same one justifies who makes: "From my mother's womb thou art my God" (Ps. 21:11). Or: **from my mother's womb**, i.e., the synagogue, whose womb is the college of Pharisees who trained him in Judaism: "You go round about the sea and the land to make one proselyte" (Mt. 23:15). Thus, therefore, was the synagogue his mother: "The sons of my mother have fought against me" (Cant. 1:5). Its womb are the Pharisees. And from this womb he was separated by the Holy Spirit unto faith in the Gospel: "Separated unto the Gospel of God" (Rom. 1:1).

Or his mother is the Church of Christ, and the womb, the college of apostles. Hence God separated him from the womb of the Church, i.e., from the college of apostles, for the office of apostleship and preacher to the Gentiles, when He said to the apostles: "Separate me Saul and Barnabas" (Ac. 13:2).

Again, he calls the synagogue his mother, because he was a Pharisee and an outstanding one, for which reason he is called a Pharisee and of the Pharisees, because he was zealous for the Law: **being more abundantly zealous for the traditions of my fathers** (v. 14).

Now as regards the other cause, he says, **and called me by his grace.** But there are two kinds of call. One is exterior, and so he says: He called me with a voice from heaven. "Saul, Saul, why persecutest thou me . . . Go into the city, and there it shall be told thee what thou must do" (Ac. 9:4). In a similar fashion He called the other apostles. The other call is interior, and in this way He calls through a certain interior instinct, whereby God touches the heart to be turned to Him, as when He calls one from the path of evil to good; and this by His grace and not our own merits: "And whom he predestinated, them he also called. And whom he called, them he also justified" (Rom. 8:30); "I have raised him up to justice" (Is. 45:13); "That calleth the waters of the sea and poureth them out upon the face of the earth: The Lord is his name" (Am. 5:8).

The end of his conversion is stated when he says, **to re-veal his Son in me.** Hence Christ is the end. Now his conver-sion is ordained to Christ in two ways: First of all, by his works. Hence he says, **to reveal his Son,** i.e., by what He did in my regard, by converting me and forgiving my sins, He revealed what a great act of mercy was bestowed on me: "Jesus Christ came into this world to save sinners, of whom I am the chief" (1 Tim. 1:15); "But I obtained the mercy of God, because I did it ignorantly in unbelief" (1 Tim. 1:13). Thus, therefore, in his conversion he revealed His Son in the sense that the Son is called the grace of God. Likewise, he revealed Him in his action; hence he says: "For I dare not speak of any of those things which Christ worketh not by me, for the obedience of the Gentiles by word and deed, by virtue of signs and wonders" (Rom. 15:18). And this inasmuch as the Son is the power [virtue] of God. Fur-thermore, he revealed Him in his preaching. Hence he said: "We preach Christ crucified; unto the Jews indeed a strumbl-ing-block, and unto the Gentiles foolishness, but unto them that are called, both Jews and Greeks, Christ, the power of God and the wisdom of God" (1 Cor. 1:23). And this inas-much as the Son is called the wisdom of God.

Secondly, his conversion is ordained to Christ by his words. Hence he says, **that I might preach him among the Gentiles,** because, whereas the other apostles preached the Gospel of Christ to the Jews, Paul, on the Lord's command, went to convert the Gentiles: "It is a small thing that thou shouldst be my servant, to raise up the tribes of Jacob and to convert the dregs of Israel. Behold, I have given thee to be the light of the Gentiles" (Is. 49:6); "For so the Lord has commanded us: that thou mayest be for salvation unto the utmost part of the earth" (Ac. 13:47); "Behold, I have given him for a witness to the people, for a leader and a master to the Gentiles" (Is. 55:4).

The manner of his conversion is perfect, both as to its effect—hence he says, **immediately I condescended not to**

flesh and blood, i.e., at once I was so completely converted
that all carnal affection left me: "It is easy in the eyes of God
on a sudden to make the poor man rich" (Ecclus. 11:23).
Flesh and blood are here taken for vices of the flesh: "Flesh
and blood cannot possess the kingdom of God" (1 Cor. 15:50).
For the flesh lusteth against the spirit (5:17). Or for the
affection and love borne toward blood relatives. "Flesh and
blood hath not revealed it to thee" (Mt. 16:17). Thus the
Apostle overcame his own vices and scorned his fellow Jews.
Furthermore, his conversion was perfect with respect to his
understanding, because he was so instructed by Christ that
there was no need to be instructed by the apostles; hence he
says, Neither went I to Jerusalem, i.e., to be instructed by
them.

Again, it was not necessary for him to be instructed by
any other of the faithful; hence he says, but I went into
Arabia. As if to say: I did not go to places where there were
believers who might instruct me, but I went to Arabia where
they were not instructed in the faith but were unbelievers.
And again I returned to Damascus, i.e., to his parents: "Who
gave a course to violent showers, or a way for noisy thunder?"
(Job 38:25).

But someone might object that it is said in Acts (9:25):
"In Damascus they let him down in a basket . . . and when
he was come into Jerusalem, he essayed to join himself to
the disciples." Therefore, according to this, he went to Jerusalem. To this I answer that he did go, but not to be instructed. Or, better still, he did not go at once but after
some time. Hence he says in the next verse, Then, after
three years I went to Jerusalem (v. 18).

# CHAPTER 1

## LECTURE 5

18 Then, after three years, I went to Jerusalem to see Peter; and I tarried with him fifteen days.

19 But other of the apostles I saw none, saving James, the brother of the Lord.

20 Now the things which I write to you, behold, before God, I lie not.

21 Afterwards, I came into the regions of Syria and Cilicia.

22 And I was unknown by face to the churches of Judea, which were in Christ;

23 But they had heard only: He, who persecuted us in times past, doth now preach the faith which once he impugned.

24 And they glorified God in me.

After showing above that he did not receive the Gospel from man before his conversion nor at the time of his conversion, the Apostle now proves that neither after his conversion did he receive it from man; but he shows, rather, how his teaching was approved by men. About this he does two things:

First, he shows how his teaching was approved by the apostles;
Secondly, he shows how it was approved by the rest of the faithful (v. 21).

First, he states the fact;
Secondly, he confirms the truth of his statement (v. 20): **before God, I lie not.**

He says therefore: Although I did not go to the apostles to be instructed by them in the beginning of my conversion, because I had already been instructed by Christ, yet, being moved by a feeling of charity, **after three years,** i.e., after my conversion, **I went to Jerusalem,** because I had long desired **to see Peter,** not to be taught by him but to visit him: "And visiting thy beauty thou shalt not sin" (Job 5:24). **And I tarried with him fifteen days,** because that number is the sum of eight and seven. Eight is the number of the New Testament, in which the eighth day of those who will rise is awaited; but seven is the number of the Old Testament, because it celebrates the seventh day. And so he stayed with Peter fifteen days, conversing with him on the mysteries of the Old and New Testament. But lest anyone suppose that although he was not instructed by Peter, he might have been instructed by others, he adds that he was not instructed by others. Hence he says, **But other of the apostles,** by whom I might be instructed, **I saw none,** i.e., no one, **saving James, the brother of the Lord.** For I saw him in Jerusalem.

Regarding James, it should be known that he was the Bishop of Jerusalem and named James the Less, because he had been called after another James. Many things are recorded of him in Acts (15:13 ff). He also wrote a canonical epistle. Now there are various explanations why he is called the brother of the Lord. Elvidius says that it was because he was the son of the Blessed Virgin. For according to him, the Blessed Virgin conceived and gave birth to Christ, and after the birth of Christ she conceived of Joseph and brought forth other sons. But this error is condemned and refuted. Furthermore, it is false for the simple reason that James was not the son of Joseph but of Alpheus.

Others say that before the Blessed Virgin, Joseph had another wife of whom he had James and other children, and that after she died, he took unto wife the Blessed Virgin, from whom Christ was born, although she was not known by Joseph, but, as it is said in the Gospel, He was conceived by the Holy Spirit. But because progeny are named after their father, and Joseph was considered the father of Christ, for that reason, James, too, although he was not the son of the Virgin, was nevertheless called the brother of the Lord.

But this is false, because if the Lord did not want as mother anyone but a virgin entrusted to the care of a virgin, how would He have allowed her husband not to be a virgin and still endure it?

Therefore others say (and this is mentioned in a Gloss) that James was the son of Mary of Cleophas, who was a sister of the Virgin. For they say that Anne, the mother of the Blessed Virgin, first married Joachim, of whom was born Mary, the mother of the Lord; but when Joachim died, she married Joachim's brother, Cleophas, from whom she bore Mary of Cleophas, and from her were born James the Less, Jude and Simon. Then after Cleophas died, she married a third man who was called Salome, of whom she conceived and bore another Mary, called Salome, from whom were born James the Great and his brother John.

But this opinion is denied on two counts by Jerome: first of all, because Salome is not a man's name, as is plain in Greek, but the name of the woman who was the sister of the Blessed Virgin and who begot James the Great and John, of Zebedee, just as Mary Cleophas begot James the Less, Jude and Simon, of Alpheus. Now this James is singled out from his other brothers and called the brother of the Lord for two reasons: first, because of a likeness in appearance, for he had a facial resemblance to Christ; and because of a likeness in their lives, for he imitated the manners of Christ. Or he is called the brother of Christ, because Alpheus, his father, was related to Joseph. Accordingly, because the Jews were accustomed to draw up the lines of ancestry on the father's side, and Christ was considered the son of Joseph, as is said in Luke (3:23), he, rather than the others, was called the brother of the Lord, because they were related to Him only on His mother's side.

Furthermore, "brother" is taken here in the sense of kinsman. For in the Scriptures some are called brothers, who are so by nature: "Jacob begot Judas and his brethren" (Mt. 1:2). Others, who are kinsmen, such as blood relations, are brothers: "Let there be no quarrel, I beseech thee, between me and thee . . . for we are brethren" (Gen. 13:8). Others who are so by race; hence all who speak the same tongue are called brothers: "Thou mayest not make a man of another nation king, that is not thy brother" (Deut. 17:15). Others who are so by affection; hence all who are friends and who have the same love are called brothers: "Because I found not Titus my brother" (2 Cor. 2:13). Others who are so by religion; hence all Christians who have one rule of life are called brothers: "For one is your master; and all you are brethren" (Mt. 23:8); "Behold how good and how pleasant it is for brethren to dwell together in unity" (Ps. 132:1). And in general, all men are called brothers, because they are ruled and protected by one God: "Have we not all one father?" (Mal. 2:10).

Then when he says, **Now the things which I write to you, behold, before God I lie not,** he confirms his statements with an oath. As if to say: The things I now write to you about myself, **behold,** are so well known that it is obvious **I lie not.** And this I say **before God,** i.e., with God as my witness. The Apostle here takes an oath not for a slight reason, but for the sake of those for whom it was necessary, that they might believe. For had he not sworn, they would not have believed him: "Before God, in Christ we speak" (2 Cor. 2:17); "God is my witness" (Rom. 1:9).

But what does the Lord say in Matthew (5:37)? "Let your speech be: Yea, Yea; No, No. And that which is over and above these is of evil." The answer to this is that it is of the evil of him who does not believe, or of the evil of punishment which compels one to swear.

Then when he says, **Afterwards, I came into the regions of Syria and Cilicia,** he shows how he was approved by the other churches of Judea. Here he does three things: first he shows where he lived, namely in Cilicia. Hence he says, **then I came into the regions of Syria and Cilicia,** i.e., his native land. (Here he was caught up into paradise). Because

it is said in Acts (22:3): "Paul was born at Tarsus in Cilicia."
Secondly, how he was known by the others, namely, not by
sight but by report and reputation. Hence he says, **I was
unknown by face to the churches of Judea, which were in
Christ,** i.e., in the faith of Christ: "As unknown and yet
known" (2 Cor. 6:8). Hence it is evident that the churches
of Judea did not teach me. **But they had heard only,** i.e.,
of me, from reports that **he who persecuted us in times past,
doth now preach the faith which once he impugned.** Thirdly,
how he was approved by them, because **they glorified God
in me,** i.e., in my conversion they glorified Him Who converted me by His grace: "The beast of the field shall glorify
me" (Is. 43:20).

# CHAPTER 2

## LECTURE 1

1 Then, after fourteen years, I went up again to Jerusalem with Barnabas, taking Titus also with me.

2 And I went up according to revelation and communicated to them the Gospel which I preach among the Gentiles; but apart to them who seemed to be something, lest perhaps I should run or had run in vain.

3 But neither Titus, who was with me, being a Gentile, was compelled to be circumcised,

4 But because of false brethren, unawares brought in, who came in privately to spy our liberty which we have in Christ Jesus, that they might bring us into servitude.

5 To whom we yielded not by subjection, no, not for an hour, that the truth of the gospel might continue with you.

After commending the authority of the Gospel teaching according to itself in the preceding chapter, the Apostle now in this chapter commends it on the part both of the other apostles and of himself. About this he does two things:

First, he commends the authority of his teaching because of its approval by the other apostles;
Secondly, from the example both of himself and of the other apostles (v. 15).

Concerning the first he does two things:

First, he shows that the other apostles approved his teaching;
Secondly, that he fearlessly rebuked the other apostles in matters where they opposed his teaching (v. 11).

As to the first he does two things:

First, he treats of the discussion he had with the apostles;

Secondly, he narrates the consequences of that discussion (v. 3).

Regarding the first he does two things:

First, he gives the circumstances of that discussion;

Secondly, what they discussed (v. 2): **and communicated to them the Gospel.**

With respect to the first he touches upon four things: first the time, then the place, the witnesses, and the motive. He mentions the time when he says, **Then, after fourteen years.** Here some might object that if the Apostle was converted in the first year after the passion of Christ, and went to Jerusalem three years later, that makes four years. But he says, **after fourteen years** I went once more to Jerusalem—which makes a total of eighteen years—at which time he found Peter in Jerusalem. But this cannot be, because Peter had his See at Antioch seven years, and then at Rome for twenty-five years. So that makes eighteen plus seven, i.e., twenty-five years, before he went to Rome, and twenty-five years more he remained there. Hence Peter would have lived for fifty years after the passion of Christ—which is false, for in the fortieth year after the passion of Christ, Peter was martyred at Rome in the reign of Nero, as is recorded in history.

I answer that when he says, **Then, after fourteen years,** it is not to be understood that after three years there was another lapse of fourteen years before he went to Jerusalem, but that he went again in the fourteenth year of his conversion. Nor should the seven years that Peter ruled the Church at Antioch be added to those fourteen years, because he began his rule before those years. Furthermore, since Antioch is near Jerusalem, Peter could at times have come to Jerusalem and Paul found him there then. Consequently, what is gathered from history is that after fourteen years Peter went

to Rome in the reign of Claudius the Emperor and lived
there for twenty-five years, making a total of thirty-nine years,
and he died in the fortieth year after the passion of Our
Lord. Yet he purposely said **fourteen** in order to show that
he did not need instructions from the apostles, if he went
for fourteen years without them.

He gives the place when he says, **Jerusalem.** And he says,
**I went up,** because it is built on a height. He went up to
Jerusalem in order to show that he was in accord with the
prophecy of Isaias (2:3): "For the law shall come forth from
Sion: and the word of the Lord from Jerusalem."

He gives the witnesses when he says, **with Barnabas, taking Titus also with me.** Now Barnabas was a Jew, but Titus
a Gentile. He went up with them, therefore, in order to have
witnesses to his teaching and to show that he leaned neither
to the side of the Jews nor the Gentiles: "In the mouth of
two or three witnesses every word shall stand" (Deut. 19:15).

He gives his motive when he says, **according to a revelation** from God, i.e., because God revealed and commanded
him to go up to Jerusalem. From this can be gathered that
all the acts and movements of the apostles were according
to an instinct of the Holy Spirit: "The clouds spread their
light which go round about" (Job 37:11).

Then when he says, **and communicated to them,** he describes the conversation. About this he does three things:

> First, he mentions the subject of their conversation;
> Secondly, the persons with whom he conferred;
> Thirdly, the reason why he conferred with them.

The subject about which he conferred was the Gospel;
hence he says, **I communicated to them the Gospel;** the persons with whom he conferred were the senior and more outstanding apostles; hence he says, **but apart to them who
seemed to be some thing.** But the reason, both useful and
necessary, was **lest I should run or had run in vain.**

Regarding the first, he says, **I went up to Jerusalem**

where **I communicated to them,** as to friends and equals,
**the Gospel which I preach among the Gentiles,** not in order
to learn, because I had already been taught by Christ, nor
in order to be reassured, because I am so certain, that if an
angel were to say the contrary, I would not believe him, as
is plain above (1:8). But I conferred for two reasons: namely,
to show the unity of my teaching with that of the other
apostles: "That you all speak the same thing and that there
be no schisms among you" (1 Cor. 1:10). Hence he conferred
with them as one having the same word as they, and not as
an adversary. Also, to avoid false accusation from others. For
the Apostle had not lived with Christ or been taught by the
apostles, but immediately after his conversion began to preach
things odious to the Jews, especially the vocation of the
Gentiles and that they should not observe the justifications
of the Law. So, then, he conferred about the Gospel.

But he indicates the ones with whom he did this, when
he adds, **but apart to them who seemed to be some thing.**
As though to say: Not with all, but with those who were of
some authority and importance among them, namely, with
Peter, James and John and the other great ones: "Treat with
the wise and prudent" (Ecclus. 9:21). **But apart,** not to talk
or treat with them about ignoble or false things, as heretics
do, but because he was aware of the presence there of Jews
who brought false charges against him for his teachings about
the Law. Hence, in order that the truth might prevail over
false charges, he spoke apart with those who would not bring
false charges against him: "Treat thy cause with thy friend,
and discover not the secret to a stranger" (Prov. 25:9); "Before a stranger do no matter of counsel: for thou knowest
not what he will bring forth" (Ecclus. 8:21). Thus the subject of the discussion as well as the persons are made known.

Then follows the cause, which was **lest perhaps I should
run or had run in vain,** i.e., lest I be thought to have preached
to no purpose. He calls his preaching a "running" on account
of the rapidity of his teaching, for in a short time he preached

the Gospel from Jerusalem to Illyricum and even as far as Spain. Hence the word of Psalm (147:15) can be said of him: "His word runneth swiftly"; "Pray, brethren, that the word of God may run and may be glorified, even as among you" (2 Thess. 3:1). But did he really wonder whether he was running in vain? I answer that he did not wonder for himself, but for those to whom he had preached, because if his teaching was not firmly held by them, he would have run in vain as far as they were concerned. So he wanted to confer with them, in order that when his hearers heard that his teaching was in agreement with that of the other apostles and approved by them, they would hold to it more firmly—then he would not be running in vain with respect to them: "I therefore so run, not as at an uncertainty" (1 Cor. 9:26).

Then when he says, **But neither Titus who was with me,** he shows what resulted from the discussion held with the apostles. And he mentions three results:

That he did not depart from his opinion;
That nothing was added to his teaching (v. 6);
Thirdly, that his teaching was approved (v. 7).

Concerning the first he does two things:

First, he shows with respect to one definite point that he did not depart from his teaching;
Secondly, that on no other point did he depart from it (v. 4).

He says, therefore: I say that the result of my discussion with them about the teaching of the Gospel was that my teaching and opinion remained unaltered concerning the non-observance of legalism, i.e., the Gentiles would not be compelled to observe the rites of the Law so that **neither Titus who was with me, being a Gentile, was compelled to be circumcised,** but was admitted uncircumcised into their fellowship by the apostles. This discussion occasioned the decree handed down by the apostles on not observing the

rites of the law, as is had in Acts (15:28). The reason why
these rites were not to be observed after the passion of Christ
is assigned in the following way by Chrysostom: "For it is
evident that the instrument drawn up for any promise or
pact binds only until the pact and promise are fulfilled; but
when fulfilled, the instrument no longer binds on that point."
Now circumcision is an instrument of the promise and pact
between God and believing men. Hence it was that Abraham
underwent circumcision as a sign of the promise, as is said
in Genesis (11:26). And because the promise was fulfilled
and the pact completed by the passion of Christ, neither the
pact holds after the passion nor is circumcision of any value.
Thus, therefore, his refusal to permit Titus to be circumcised
makes it plain that he did not depart from his teaching.

Then when he says, **but because of false brethren, unawares brought in,** he shows that he did not change on any
other point. This passage is obscure and variant readings
are found. It should be read thus: You say that you did not
permit Titus to be circumcised; but why? seeing that in another case you permitted Timothy, as is read in Acts (16:3).
To this the Apostle can respond that when Timothy was circumcised, it was an indifferent matter whether circumcision
was observed or not; but later on, when it came to Titus,
circumcision became a matter of paramount importance and
I said that it is not to be observed. Hence, if I had allowed
him to be circumcised, whereas I had already settled the
question definitively myself, I would have been acting to
the contrary. Furthermore, it was not lawful to raise this
question again or to make difficulties about a matter now
settled.

He says therefore: I say that I did not permit him to
be circumcised by them, **to whom we yielded not by subjection, no, not for an hour,** i.e., that the Gentiles be subject
to the Law; and this **because of false brethren, unawares
brought in** by the devil or by the Pharisees: **false brethren,**
because they pretended to be friends: "In perils from false

brethren" (2 Cor. 11:26). **Who,** namely the false brethren, **were brought into** the place where the apostles were gathered, **in order to spy on our liberty** from sin and the Law: "Where the Spirit of the Lord is, there is liberty" (2 Cor. 3:17); "You have not received the spirit of bondage again in fear; but you have received the spirit of the adoption of sons" (Rom. 8:15); **that he might redeem them who were under the Law** (4:5). **Which** liberty we have in Christ Jesus, i.e., through faith in Christ: **You are not children of the bondwoman but of the free** (4:31). And to this end were they brought in, **that they might bring us into servitude** of the Law and the observances of the flesh, as before the passion of Christ. But this is not permissible, "for other foundation no man can lay, but that which is laid; which is Christ Jesus" (1 Cor. 3:11). And this, **that the truth of the gospel might continue with you.** As if to say: We did not yield to them an iota, lest we give an occasion to those who said that you cannot be saved without circumcision, which is contrary to the truth of the Gospel I have preached to you.

Ambrose, however, reads it another way. For according to the foregoing the reason he did not yield for the moment was on account of those brought in. From this it follows that if they had not been brought in, he would have yielded in the matter of observing legalism. Therefore it was not on that account, because on that account he would not have yielded to them, but on account of the truth itself. Therefore, says Ambrose, the text is faulty and the words, **no not even,** are superfluous. Hence he would have it that those words should not be there. And then the sense is: I did not permit Titus to be circumcised, but Timothy I did, **because of false brethren, unawares brought in,** i.e., to the place where I was with Timothy and the others **who were brought in to spy our liberty.** But when they failed in this, they tried to incite the people to rise up against us. **To whom,** i.e., to the false brethren, we therefore **yielded in the hour of subjection** in the matter of circumcision by circumcising Timothy,

in order that the truth of the gospel might continue with
you, i.e., the Gospel which teaches that neither circumcision
nor uncircumcision profits anything, but the faith.

But the special reason why Timothy was circumcised and
Titus not, was that Timothy was born of a Gentile father
and Jewish mother, whereas Titus' parents were both Gentiles. And the opinion of the Apostle was that those born of
a Jewish parent on either side should be circumcised, but
those born entirely of Gentile parents should on no account
be circumcised.

# CHAPTER 2

## LECTURE 2

6 But of them who seemed to be something, (what they were
some time, it is nothing to me, God accepteth not the person of man);
for to me they that seemed to be something added nothing.
7 But contrariwise, when they had seen that to me was committed
the gospel of the uncircumcision, as to Peter was that of the circumcision,
8 (For he who wrought in Peter to the apostleship of the circumcision wrought in me also among the Gentiles.)
9 And, when they had known the grace that was given to me,
James and Cephas and John, who seemed to be pillars, gave to me
and Barnabas the right hands of fellowship; that we should go unto
the Gentiles, and they unto the circumcision;
10 Only that we should be mindful of the poor; which same thing
also I was careful to do.

Having shown that the Apostle did not depart from his
opinion on any point in the conference mentioned above, he
now shows that nothing was added to his teaching by the
other apostles. About this he does two things:

First, he describes the status of the apostles who were
unable to add anything;

Secondly, he proves his proposition (v. 6): **for to me, they that seemed to be something, added nothing.**

Their status he describes from three standpoints: first from the authority they held in the Church, for it was great. Regarding it he says, **But of them who seemed to be some thing.** The text is deficient and should be amended to read, "But of them," namely, Peter and John. As if to say: Although I would have yielded to them at the time, yet I received from them no new power or teaching. And if I received nothing from them, much less so from others. But it is to be noted that if his statement, **who seemed to be something,** is understood with reference to the grace of God that was in them, it is true that in this respect they were great, because "whom he justified, them he also glorified," as is said in Romans (8:30). However, if it is understood that they were something according to themselves, then it is false, because in that respect they were nothing. For if they seemed to be some thing according to themselves, they would always have been great, because whatever belongs to a thing according to itself is always present. Hence, since they were not always great, it was not according to themselves that they were seen to be something.

Secondly, he describes their status on the side of what they were before their conversion, i.e., the status they had in the synagogue. This status, he hints gently, was mean and lowly. Hence he says, **what they were some time;** for they had been coarse, poor, ignorant and unlettered: "There are not many wise according to the flesh, not many mighty, not many noble" (1 Cor. 1:26). **But what they were is nothing to me,** i.e., it is not my concern to mention. Perhaps his reason for introducing this was that by considering the status they had in the synagogue—which was nothing—and the status of Paul—which was great—they might see that Paul's opinion on legalism should be preferred to theirs, particularly since Paul has an equal status with them in the Church;

so that Paul had a higher rank in the synagogue before their conversion, but after the conversion, he had a rank equal to theirs. Hence when matters concerning the synagogue were discussed, the opinion of Paul deserved to prevail over the others, but when it came to the Gospel, his opinion was as good as theirs. And just as the others were not made great through things pertaining to the Law but through Christ, so too in the faith the Apostle was great through Christ and not through things pertaining to the Law.

Thirdly, he describes their condition by reason of their election by God. Regarding this he says, **God accepteth not the person.** As if to say: They are great because God made them great, not by regarding their merits or demerits, but by regarding what He intended to accomplish. Hence he says: **God accepteth not the person of man,** i.e., he does not consider whether the person is great or little: "For he made the little and the great, and he hath equally care of all" (Wis. 6:8). Furthermore, without regard to person, He calls everyone to salvation, no longer charging them with their sins for they have passed away: "The old things are passed away" (2 Cor. 5:17); "Nor will I be mindful of their name" (Ps. 15:5). Therefore Peter says: "In very deed I perceive that God is not a respecter of persons" (Ac. 10:34).

On this point it should be noted that accepting of persons in any transaction is, properly speaking, to take as a deciding factor in that transaction some aspect of the person that has nothing to do with the matter; for example, when I give a benefice to a person just because he is a noble or is handsome. For nobility or beauty have nothing to do with the question of getting a benefice. But if some aspect of the person does have something to do with the matter, then if I consider that aspect in settling the matter, I do not accept the person; for example, if I give a benefice to a person because he is good and will serve the Church well, or because he is well-educated and honorable, I am not an acceptor of persons. Therefore to accept the person is nothing other than to consider some aspect of the person that has no relation to the business. Hence, since God in His works and benefits regards nothing that pre-exists on the side of the creature—for that which pertains to the creature is an effect of His election—but takes as His measure merely what pleases His will, according to which He effects all things, and not the condition of their person, as is said in Ephesians (1:11), it is evident that He does not regard the person of man.

Then, having described their condition, he proves his proposition, namely, that they were unable to add anything to him. Hence he says, **for to me they that seemed to be something added nothing.** As if to say: Although they had great authority, they added nothing to my teaching or to my power, because, as was said above, I neither received the Gospel from man nor learned it by man.

However, a certain Gloss has a different reading, namely, **what they were at one time is not my concern.** As if to say: It is not my concern to recount their status before their conversion, i.e., what they were, because this too makes no difference, since I myself had even been a persecutor of that Church; yet God by the pleasure of His will chose and glorified me—and this because the Lord does not regard the person of man.

Then when he says, **But contrariwise, when they had seen . . . ,** he shows how his opinion was approved by the apostles. About this he does three things:

First, he gives the reason for this approbation;
Secondly, he mentions the approbation (v. 9); **James and Cephas and John, who seemed to be pillars, gave to me and Barnabas the right hands of fellowship;**
Thirdly, he adds a condition that was placed on the approbation (v. 10).

He cites the two causes of the approbation (which moved the apostles to approve the opinion of the Apostle) namely, the office of teaching enjoined by Christ on the Apostle; and the effect of this appointment (v. 9). As to the first, he does two things:

First, he mentions the office to which he was appointed which moved them to approve him;
Secondly, the manifestation of this office (v. 8).

He says therefore: I say that those **who seemed to be something, added nothing;** but rather, contrary to the opinion of the adversaries who came up to Jerusalem to oppose me in this matter, it was I that the Apostles approved, and this **when they had seen that to me was committed the gospel,** i.e., the office of the preaching, **of the uncircumcision,** i.e., the injunction to preach to the uncircumcised, namely, the Gentiles: "For all the nations are uncircumcised in the flesh, but all the house of Israel are uncircumcised in the heart" (Jer. 9:26). Just as to Peter was entrusted the authority to preach to the Jews alone, so to Paul to the Gentiles; but later, Peter, too, preached to the Gentiles and Paul to the Jews.

But because someone might say: What evidence have you that the commission to preach the Gospel to the Gentiles was given you, he interjects that it was through certain works of Christ. For just as it is evident that Peter received the Gospel from Christ because of the marvels Christ wrought through him, so it is evident that I received it because of the miracles Christ worked and does work in me. Therefore he says, **He who wrought in Peter to the apostleship,** i.e., made Peter an apostle in Judea, namely Christ, also made me an apostle among the Gentiles. And this is the reason which moves them.

But because one's appointment and authority to preach are not enough, unless he carries it out through good understanding and discreet eloquence and commends it by a good life, he adds how he used his authority or the effect

of his office, saying, **And, when they had known the grace
of God that was given to me, James and Cephas and John
. . . gave to me and Barnabas, the right hands of fellowship.** This is a dependent clause, i.e., when they saw that
my preaching enjoyed favor and was fruitful, **James and
Cephas and John, who seemed to be pillars . . .** In this passage is mentioned the approval or fellowship entered into
by them and Paul. First, the persons are mentioned with
whom the fellowship was formed, namely, James and Cephas,
i.e., Peter, and John. James is mentioned first, as being the
Bishop of Jerusalem where these events took place. The John
mentioned was John the Evangelist who did not quit Judea
until the time of Vespasian.

**Who seem to be pillars.** This is a metaphor standing for
"the support of the entire Church." For just as a whole
edifice is supported by the pillars, so the whole Church of
the Jews was supported and governed by these men. Of
those pillars it is said in Psalm (74:4): "I have established
the pillars thereof," i.e., the apostles of the Church; "His legs
as pillars of marble, that are set upon bases of gold" (Cant.
5:15). **They,** on the one side, **gave the right hands of fellowship,** i.e., consented to the fellowship, **to me and Barnabas,** the persons on the other side. By giving them their right
hands they signified that they accepted them into their hands
as a sign of union and unity of opinion.

Secondly, the intent or condition of the fellowship is
shown when it is said, **that we should go unto the Gentiles,
and they unto the circumcision,** i.e., to preach. As if to say:
A bond and union was made among us to the effect that just
as the faithful obey Peter among the circumcision, i.e., in
the Church of the Jewish believers, so all the Gentiles converted to Christ should obey Paul and Barnabas. But they
added the condition **that we should be mindful of the poor
of Christ,** i.e., of those who had sold all their goods and
laid the price at the feet of the apostles and became poor
for the sake of Christ. **Which same thing, indeed, also I was**

**careful to do,** being no less moved than those commanding me, as is plain in Romans (Ch. 15), 1 Corinthians (Ch. 6) and 2 Corinthians (Ch. 8 and 9).

Now the reason why the custom prevailed in the early Church for those in the Church of the circumcision to sell their goods and not those in the Church of the Gentiles was that the believing Jews were congregated in Jerusalem and in Judea, which was soon to be destroyed by the Romans, as later events proved. Hence the Lord willed that no possessions were to be kept in a place not destined to endure. But the Church of the Gentiles was destined to grow strong and increase, and therefore, by the inspiration of the Holy Spirit, it came about that the possessions in it were not to be sold.

# CHAPTER 2

## LECTURE 3

11 But, when Cephas was come to Antioch, I withstood him to the face, because he was to be blamed.

12 For, before that some came from James, he did eat with the Gentiles; but, when they were come, he withdrew and separated himself, fearing them who were of the circumcision.

13 And to his dissimulation the rest of the Jews consented; so that Barnabas also was led by them into that dissimulation.

14 But, when I saw that they walked not uprightly unto the truth of the gospel, I said to Cephas before them all: If thou, being a Jew, livest after the manner of the Gentiles and not as the Jews do, how dost thou compel the Gentiles to live as do the Jews?

The Apostle showed above that he received nothing useful from the discussion held with the apostles; now he shows that he benefited them:

First, he shows how he helped Peter by correcting him; Secondly, he tells what he said (v. 12).

He says, therefore: Indeed, they advantaged me nothing; rather I conferred something upon them, and especially upon Peter, because **when Cephas was come to Antioch,** where there was a church of the Gentiles, **I withstood him to the face,** i.e., openly: "Reverence not thy neighbor in his fall and refrain not to speak in the time of salvation" (Ecclus. 4:27). Or: **to his face,** i.e., not in secret as though detracting and fearing him, but publicly and as his equal: "Thou shalt not hate thy brother in thy heart: but reprove him openly, lest thou incur sin through him" (Lev. 19:17). This he did, **because he was to be blamed.**

But it might be objected: This took place after they received the grace of the Holy Spirit; but after the grace of the Holy Spirit the apostles did not sin in any way. I answer that after the grace of the Holy Spirit the apostles did not sin mortally, and this gift they had through the divine power that had strengthened them: "I have established the pillars thereof" (Ps. 74:4). Yet they sinned venially because of human frailty: "If we say that we have no sin," i.e., venial, "we deceive ourselves" (1 John 1:8).

Apropos of what is said in a certain Gloss, namely, that **I withstood him** as an adversary, the answer is that the Apostle opposed Peter in the exercise of authority, not in his authority of ruling. Therefore from the foregoing we have an example: prelates, indeed, an example of humility, that they not disdain corrections from those who are lower and subject to them; subjects have an example of zeal and freedom, that they fear not to correct their prelates, particularly if their crime is public and verges upon danger to the multitude.

Then when he says, **For, before that some came from James,** he manifests what he has said.

First, that he said he was to be blamed;
Secondly, that he rebuked Peter (v. 14).

As to the first he does three things:

First, he shows what Peter's opinion was;
Secondly, what he did (v. 11);
Thirdly, what resulted from it (v. 13).

He says therefore, as to the first point, that Peter felt that
legalism ought not be observed. This he showed by the fact
that **before some came,** namely, Jews zealous for the Law,
**from James,** Bishop of the Church at Jerusalem, **he did eat,**
namely, Peter did, **with the Gentiles,** i.e., without compunc-
tion he ate the food of Gentiles. He did this through the
inspiration of the Holy Spirit Who had said to him: "That
which God hath cleansed, do not thou call common," as is
had in Acts (10:15), and as he himself in the following
chapter said in answer to the Jews who rose up against him,
because he had eaten with the uncircumcised.

What Peter did Paul now shows, saying that when he
was with the Jews, **he withdrew** from the company of the
faithful who had been converted from the Gentiles and ad-
hered to the Jews alone and mingled among them. Therefore
he says, **but when they were come,** namely, from Judea, Peter
**withdrew** from the converted Gentiles **and separated himself**
from them. This he did because he was **fearing them who
were of the circumcision,** i.e., the Jews, not with a human
or worldly fear but a fear inspired by charity, namely, lest
they be scandalized, as is said in a Gloss. Hence he became
to the Jews as a Jew, pretending that he felt the same as
they did in their weakness. Yet he feared unreasonably, because the truth must never be set aside through fear of scandal.

What resulted from this dissimulation he mentions when
he says that **to his dissimulation,** i.e., Peter's, **the rest of the
Jews consented** who were at Antioch, discriminating between
food and separating themselves from the Gentiles, although
prior to this act of dissimulation they would not have done
this. And not only they consented to Peter, but such was
the effect of that dissimulation upon the hearts of the faithful, **that Barnabas also,** who along with me was a teacher

of the Gentiles and had done and taught the contrary, **was
led by them into that dissimulation** and withdrew from them,
namely, the Gentiles. And this on account of what is said in
Ecclesiasticus (10:2): "What manner of man the ruler of a
city is, such also are they that dwell therein" and "as the
judge of the people is himself, so also are his ministers."

Then when he says, **But, when I saw that they walked
not uprightly unto the truth of the gospel, I said to Cephas
before them all . . . ,** he explains what he had said concerning the rebuke with which he rebuked Peter. As to this he
does three things:

First, he gives the reason for the rebuke;
Secondly, the manner of rebuking;
Thirdly, the words of the rebuke.

The occasion of the rebuke was not slight, but just and
useful, namely, the danger to the Gospel teaching. Hence he
says: Thus was Peter reprehensible, but I alone, **when I
saw that they,** who were doing these things, **walked not uprightly unto the truth of the gospel,** because its truth was
being undone, if the Gentiles were compelled to observe the
legal justifications, as will be plain below. That they were
not walking uprightly is so, because in cases where danger
is imminent, the truth must be preached openly and the opposite never condoned through fear of scandalizing others:
"That which I tell you in the dark, speak ye in the light"
(Mt. 10:27); "The way of the just is right: the path of the
just is right to walk in" (Is. 26:7). The manner of the rebuke
was fitting, i.e., public and plain. Hence he says, **I said to
Cephas,** i.e., to Peter, **before them all,** because that dissimulation posed a danger to all: "Them that sin, reprove before
all" (1 Tim. 5:20). This is to be understood of public sins
and not of private ones, in which the procedures of fraternal
charity ought to be observed.

The words the Apostle spoke to Peter when he rebuked
him, he adds, saying, **If thou, being a Jew,** by nature and

race, **livest after the manner of the Gentiles and not as the Jews do,** i.e., if you observe the customs of Gentiles and not of Jews, since you know and feel that discriminating among foods is of no importance, **how dost thou compel the Gentiles,** not indeed by command, but by example of your behavior, **to live as do the Jews?** He says, **compel,** because as Pope Leo says, "Example has more force than words." Hence Paul rebukes Peter precisely because he had been instructed by God that although he had previously lived as the Jews do, he should no longer discriminate among foods: "That which God hath cleansed, do not thou call common" (Ac. 10:15). But now Peter was dissembling the opposite.

It should be noted that these words occasioned no small controversy between Jerome and Augustine and, as their writings clearly show, they are seen to disagree on four points. First, as to the time of the legal justifications, namely, when they should have been observed. For Jerome distinguishes two periods, one before the passion of Christ and one after. Jerome's opinion is that the legal justifications were *living* before the passion of Christ, i.e., had validity, inasmuch as original sin was removed through circumcision, and God was pleased with sacrifices and victims. But after the passion they were, according to him, not only not living i.e., dead, but what is more, they were *deadly,* so that whoever observed them after the passion of Christ sinned mortally.

Augustine, on the other hand, distinguishes three periods. One period was before the passion of Christ and, in agreement with Jerome, he says that during that period the legal justifications were *living.* Another was the period immediately following the passion of Christ, before grace was promulgated (as the time of the apostles in the beginning); during this period, says Augustine, the legal justifications were *dead* but not yet *deadly* to the converted Jews, so long as the ones observing them placed no hope in them. Hence the Jews observed them during that period without sinning. But had they placed their trust in them when observing them after their conversion, they would have sinned mortally; because if they placed their trust in them so as to believe that they were necessary for salvation, then, as far as they were concerned, they would have been voiding the grace of Christ. Finally, he posits a third period, after the truth and grace of Christ had been proclaimed. It was during that period, he says, that they were both *dead* and *deadly* to all who observed them.

The reasoning that underlies these statements is that if the Jews had been forbidden the legal observances right after their conversion, it might have seemed that they had previously been on an equal footing with idolaters, who were immediately forbidden to worship idols, and that just as idolatry had never been good, so too the legal observances. Therefore, under the inspiration of the Holy Spirit, the legal observances were condoned for a short time for the reason given, namely, to show that the legal observances had been good in the past. Hence, says Augustine, the fact that the legal justifications were not forbidden right after the passion of Christ showed that the mother, the synagogue, was destined to be brought in honor to the grave. But whosoever did not observe them in that manner would not be honoring the mother, the synagogue, but disturbing her grave.

Secondly, the aforesaid Jerome and Augustine disagree on the observance of the legal justifications with respect to the apostles. For Jerome says that the apostles never really observed them but pretended to do so, in order to avoid scandalizing the believers who had been of the circumcision. He says that even Paul made this pretense when he fulfilled a vow in the temple at Jerusalem, as is narrated in Acts (21:26), and when he circumcised Timothy, as in Acts (16:3), and when on advice from James he observed some of the justifications, as recorded in Acts (20:20). But in so doing the apostles were not misleading the faithful, because they did not act with the intention of observing the justifications but for other reasons; for example, they rested on the Sabbath, not because it was a legal observance, but for the sake of rest. Likewise, they abstained from food legally unclean, not for the sake of observing the legal justifications but for other reasons; for example, on account of an abhorrence or something of that nature. But Augustine says that the apostles observed the legal justifications and intended to do so, but without putting their trust in them as though they were necessary for salvation. Furthermore, this was lawful for them to do, because they had been Jews. Nevertheless, they observed them before grace was proclaimed. Hence just as certain other Jews could safely observe them at that time without putting any trust in them, so too could the apostles.

Thirdly, they disagree on the sin of Peter. For Jerome says that in the dissimulation previously mentioned, Peter did not sin, because he did this from charity and, as has been said, not from mundane fear. Augustine, on the other hand, says, that he did sin—venially, however—on account of the lack of discretion he had by adhering overmuch to one side, namely, to the Jews, in order to avoid scandalizing them. But the stronger of Augustine's arguments against Jerome is that Jerome adduces on his own behalf seven doctors, four of whom, namely, Laudicens, Alexander, Origen, and Didymus, Augustine rejects as known heretics. To the other three he opposes three of his own, who held with him and his opinion, namely, Ambrose, Cyprian, and Paul himself, who plainly teaches that Peter was deserving of rebuke. Therefore, if it is unlawful to say that anything false is contained in Sacred Scripture, it will not be lawful to say that Peter was not deserving of rebuke. For this reason the opinion and statement of Augustine is the truer, because it is more in accord with the words of the Apostle.

Fourthly, they disagree on Paul's rebuke. For Jerome says that Paul did not really rebuke Peter but pretended to do so, just as Peter pretended to observe the legal justifications, i.e. just as Peter in his unwillingness to scandalize the Jews pretended to observe the justifications, so Paul, in order not to scandalize the Gentiles, feigned displeasure at Peter's action and pretended to rebuke him. This was done, as it were, by mutual consent, so that each might exercise his care over the believers subject to them. Augustine, however, just as he says that Peter really did observe the justifications, says that Paul truly rebuked him without pretense. Furthermore, Peter really sinned by observing them, because his action was a source of scandal to the Gentiles from whom he separated himself. But Paul did not sin in rebuking him, because no scandal followed from his rebuke.

# CHAPTER 2

## LECTURE 4

15 We by nature are Jews; and not of the Gentiles, sinners.
16 But knowing that man is not justified by the works of the law, but by the faith of Jesus Christ, we also believe in Christ Jesus, that we may be justified by the faith of Christ and not by the works of the law; because by the works of the law no flesh shall be justified.

Having manifested the truth of the apostolic doctrine preached by him because of the authority of the other apostles, he now shows the same thing from their manner of life and example. About this he does two things:

First, he proves his proposition from the manner of life of the apostles;
Secondly, he raises an objection posed by his adversaries (v. 17).

As to the first he does three things:

First, he sets forth the status of the apostles;
Secondly, their manner of life (v. 16);
Thirdly, the intended conclusion: (v. 16): **because by the works of the law no flesh shall be justified.**

The status of the apostles and even of Paul is that according to natural origin they were born Jews. That is why he says, **We,** namely, I and the other apostles, are **by nature,** i.e. by natural origin, **Jews,** not proselytes: "They are Hebrews: so am I" (2 Cor. 11:22). And this is a great compliment, because, as it is said: "Salvation is of the Jews" (Jn. 4:22). **And not of the Gentiles, sinners,** i.e., we are not sinners as are the Gentiles, idolatrous and unclean.

But against this can be set the word of 1 John (1:8): "If we say that we have no sin, we deceive ourselves." Therefore, the Jews were sinners. I answer that it is one thing to sin and another to be a sinner. For the first names an act, but the second a readiness or habit of sinning. Hence Scripture is wont to call the impious and those loaded down with the heavy burden of sin, sinners. The Jews therefore, being haughty on account of the Law, and as it were, restrained from sin by it, called the Gentiles sinners, living as they were without the Laws' restraint and being prone to sin: "Be no more carried about with every wind of doctrine" (Eph. 4:14). When, therefore, the Apostle says, **not of the Gentiles, sinners,** he means we are not of that number of sinners that exist among the Gentiles.

Then when he says, **But knowing that man is not justified by the works . . .** he sets forth the apostles' manner of life, which consists not in the works of the Law but in the faith of Christ. About this he does two things:

> First, he gives the reason for the apostles' manner of
> life;
> Secondly, he sets forth their manner of life (v. 16): **we**
> **also believe in Christ Jesus.**

Therefore the apostolic life rested on the faith of Christ and not on the works of the Law. The reason for this is that although we were Jews by nature and were nourished in the works of the Law, yet **knowing** for certain **that man is not justified by the works of the law,** i.e., through the works of

the Law, **but by the faith of Jesus Christ,** for that reason
we have left the Law and are living according to the precepts of the faith: "For we account a man to be justified by
faith, without the works of the Law" (Rom. 3:28); "For
there is no other name under heaven given to men whereby
we must be saved" (Ac. 4:12).

However, it is said in Romans (2:13): "For not the
hearers of the law are just before God; but the doers of the
law shall be justified." Therefore, it seems that a man would
be justified by the works of the Law. I answer that "to be
justified" can be taken in two senses, namely, doing what is
just, and being made just. But no one is made just save by
God through grace. It should be known, therefore, that some
works of the Law were moral and some ceremonial. The
moral, although they were contained in the Law, could not,
strictly speaking, be called "works of the Law," for man is
induced to them by natural instinct and by the natural law.
But the ceremonial works are properly called the "works of
the Law." Therefore, to that extent is man justified by the
moral laws—so far as the execution of justice is concerned—
and also by the ceremonial laws that pertain to the sacraments, as their observance is a work of obedience. And this
is the way it is taken in the word of the Apostle to the
Romans (2:13).

But with respect to being made just by the works of
the Law, a man does not seem to be justified by them, because the sacraments of the Old Law did not confer grace.
**How turn you again to the weak and needy elements?** i.e.,
that neither confer grace nor contain grace in themselves.
The sacraments of the New Law however, although they are
material elements, are not needy elements; hence they can
justify. Again, if there were any in the Old Law who were
just, they were not made just by the works of the Law but
only by the faith of Christ "Whom God hath proposed to
be a propitiation through faith," as is said in Romans (3:25).
Hence the sacraments of the Old Law were certain protesta-

tions of the faith of Christ, just as our sacraments are, but not in the same way, because those sacraments were configured to the grace of Christ as to something that lay in the future; our sacraments, however, testify as things containing a grace that is present. Therefore, he says significantly, that **it is not by the works of the law that we are justified, but by the faith of Christ,** because, although some who observed the works of the Law in times past were made just, nevertheless, this was effected only by the faith of Jesus Christ.

From this knowledge which the apostles had, namely, that justification is not by the works of the Law but by the faith of Christ, he concludes to their manner of life, in which they chose the faith of Christ and gave up the works of the Law. Hence he adds, **we also believe in Christ Jesus,** because as is said in Acts (4:12): "There is no other name under heaven given to men, whereby we must be saved." Therefore he continued, **that we may be justified by the faith of Christ.** "Being justified, therefore, by faith, let us have peace with God" (Rom. 5:1). But lest anyone suppose that the works of the Law along with the faith of Christ justify, he adds, **and not by the works of the law:** "For we account a man to be justified by faith, without the works of the Law" (Rom. 3:28).

From this he derives his main proposition, saying that if the apostles, who are Jews by nature, do not seek to be justified by the works of the Law but by faith, then **by the works of the law no flesh shall be justified,** i.e., no man whatsoever can be justified by the works of the Law. For "flesh" is taken here to stand for "man," i.e., the part for the whole, as does "All flesh shall see the salvation of the Lord" (Is. 40:5). Then by saying, **because by the works of the law no flesh shall be justified,** he concludes, as it were, *a fortiori.* For it seems more natural or reasonable for the Jews, more than anyone else, to be justified by the works of the Law rather than by faith. But this is not the case. Therefore . . .

# CHAPTER 2

## LECTURE 5

17 But if, while we seek to be justified in Christ, we ourselves also are found sinners, is Christ then the minister of sin? God forbid!
18 For, if I build up again the things which I have destroyed, I make myself a prevaricator.

After proving by the apostles' manner of life that the works of the Law ought not to be observed, the Apostle raises a question to the contrary. About this he does three things:

First, he raises the question;
Secondly, he solves it (v. 17): **God forbid;**
Thirdly, he explains his solution (v. 19).

The first point can be developed in two ways according to a Gloss. First, thus: Someone could say that the apostles sinned by abandoning the Law and turning to the faith of Christ. But the Apostle shows that this would lead to the following unwelcome conclusion, namely, that Christ is the author of sin in calling men to His faith. This is what he means when he says, **But if,** we apostles, **while we seek to be justified in him,** i.e., through Him, namely, Christ, **are found,** i.e., plainly proven to be **sinners** for leaving the Law, **is Christ then the minister of sin?** i.e., is He inducing us to sin, Who called us from the slavery of the Law to His faith? **Made under the law that he might redeem them that were under the law** (4:4), namely, from the burden of the Law.
The Apostle answers, **God forbid,** because He is rather the minister of justice; "By the obedience of one, many shall be made just" (Rom. 5:19); "Who did no sin, neither was

guile found in his mouth" (1 Pet. 2:22). That Christ is not
the minister of sin in leading one from the Old Law is plain,
because if I myself, by wanting to glory once more in the
Law, **build up again** the things **I have destroyed,** namely,
my pride taking glory in the Law, **I make myself a prevaricator** in taking up what I destroyed: "The dog is returned
to his vomit" (2 Pet. 2:22); "Cursed be the man that shall
raise up and build the city of Jericho" (Jos. 6:26). He says,
**which I have destroyed,** i.e., not the Law itself, as the Man-
icheans would have it, because the Law is holy (Rom. 7:12),
but pride in the Law, concerning which it is said in Romans
(10:3): "For they, seeking to establish their own justice have
not submitted themselves to the justice of God."

Now if someone were to object that since he formerly
had wasted the faith of Christ, he makes himself a prevaricator by trying to build it up, the plain answer is that he
did indeed try to destroy the faith of Christ, yet because
of the truth he did not persist: "Why persecutest thou me?
It is hard for thee to kick against the goad" (Ac. 9:4). But
pride in the Law was vain and this pride could be destroyed,
never again to be re-established.

The second way in which it can be developed is to refer his statement, **we ourselves are found sinners,** not to their
abandoning the Law, as in the first explanation, but to the
observance of the Law. For it is plain that anyone who seeks
to be made just does not profess himself to be just but a
sinner. The sense, therefore, is this: **if we, in seeking to be
justified in Christ, are** by the very fact of seeking to be
justified **found,** i.e., reasonably proved, to have been **sinners,**
because we observed the Law, **is Jesus Christ then the minister of sin?** i.e., commanding men to observe the works of the
Law after His passion—something that cannot be done without sin? Note that this explanation harmonizes with Jerome's
opinion which posited that the legal justifications were deadly
immediately after the passion of Christ.

It is possible to explain, **we ourselves are found to be**

**sinners,** in a third way as referring, indeed, to the state in which the Law was observed; not that they offended by observing the Law, but that the Law is deficient and cannot remove sin. Hence the meaning is this: If in seeking to be justified in it, we ourselves are found to be sinners, i.e., still in our sins, because the Law does not remove sin—according to Romans (3:9): "For we have charged both Jews and Greeks, that they are all under sin"—**Is Jesus Christ then the minister of sin,** so as to bring us back to observing the Law in which we are under sin? This explanation accords with Augustine's exposition.

And he [Paul] answers to either explanation, **God forbid,** because I destroyed the Law understood carnally by judging and teaching it spiritually. Hence, if I should desire to re-establish the observances of the carnal law, I would be a prevaricator of the spiritual law.

Furthermore, it can be explained in a fourth way, thus: I had said that man is not justified by the works of the Law. But someone might say, "Nor by the faith of Christ either," because many sin after embracing the faith of Christ. And this is what he says: **If we, seeking to be justified in Christ,** i.e., by the faith of Christ, **are ourselves,** who have become believers by embracing the faith of Christ, **found to be sinners,** i.e., living in sin, **is Jesus Christ then the minister of sin** and of damnation, as the minister of the Old Law is a minister of sin and damnation? Not that the Law led one into sin, but was its occasion, because it forbade sin and conferred no grace to help one resist sin. Hence it is said: "But sin, taking occasion by the commandment, wrought in me all manner of concupiscence" (Rom. 7:8). But Christ gives a helping grace: "Grace and truth came by Jesus Christ" (Jn. 1:17). Hence in no way is He the minister of sin, either directly or as its occasion.

# CHAPTER 2

## LECTURE 6

19 For I, through the law, am dead to the law, that I may live to God; with Christ I am nailed to the cross.

20 And I live, now not I; but Christ liveth in me. And that I live now in the flesh, I live in the faith of the Son of God, who loved me and delivered himself for me.

21 I cast not away the grace of God. For if justice be by the law, then Christ died in vain.

Here the Apostle amplifies the solution given above. First, he explains the solution. Secondly, he concludes to his principal proposition (v. 21). It should be noted that the Apostle proceeds in a very thorough manner, leaving no doubt unexamined. Hence his words, although they seem involved, nevertheless, if they are carefully considered, say nothing without a purpose. This is plain from the words he uses. Therefore, he does three things:

First, he manifests the solution;
Secondly, he explains his manifestation of the solution; (v. 19): **with Christ I am nailed to the cross;**
Thirdly, he settles the question (v. 20): **That I live now in the flesh.**

Therefore, because the Apostle had said, **For, if I build up again the things which I have destroyed,** which is understood to refer to the Old Law, for one might regard him as a destroyer of the Law and consequently impious according to Psalm (118:126): "They have dissipated thy law," for that reason the Apostle wishes to show how he destroys the Law without being impious, saying, **For I, through the law, am dead to the law.** Here it should be noted that when anyone destroys a law by means of the law itself, he is indeed a prevaricator of the law, but not impious. For a law is destroyed by means of the law when the law itself contains some local or temporary precept, such that the law should be observed for such a time or in such a place and no other, and this fact is expressed in the law. If someone, therefore, after that time or outside that place, does not use the law, he destroys the law by means of the law itself, and in this way the Apostle destroyed the Law. Hence he says: I somehow destroyed the Law, but by means of the Law; because **through the Law I am dead to the Law,** i.e., by the authority of the Law I have rejected the Law, as being dead to the Law. For the authority of the Law, through which he is dead to the Law, is cited in many places in Sacred Scripture. For example, although not in so many words, it is had in Jeremias (31:31): "I will make a new covenant with the house of Israel"; "The Lord will raise up to thee a prophet of thy brethren like unto me" (Deut. 18:15), and in many other places. Therefore the Apostle is not a destroyer of the Law in the sense of a transgressor of the Law.

Or else, **I by the law** spiritual **am dead to the law** carnal. For he dies to the Law when, being freed by the Law, he casts it aside, according to Romans (7:2): "If her husband be dead, she is loosed from the law of her husband." Now inasmuch as the Apostle was subject to the spiritual law, he says that he is dead to the Law, i.e., loosed from the observances of the Law: "For the law of the spirit of life, in Christ Jesus, hath delivered me from the law of sin and of death" (Rom. 8:2). Again there is another possible way of setting the law aside without prevarication, because, namely, a law, when it is written on a scroll is called a dead law, and when it is in the mind of the lawgiver it is called a living law. Now it is plain that if someone were to act according to the word of the lawgiver against the written law and break the law, he would both be set free of the dead law and be acting according to the command of the lawgiver.

He says, therefore, along these lines, **I am dead to the law,** which is written and dead, i.e., I am loosed from it **that I may live to God,** i.e., that I may guide my movements according to His precepts and be ordained to His honor. For a law that has been passed does, indeed, hand down something in writing on account of those outside and of those who cannot hear the words spoken by the lawgiver; but for those in his presence he does not lay it down in writing but in words alone. For in the beginning, men were weak and unable to approach unto God; hence it was necessary for the precepts of the Law to be given to them in writing, so that by the Law, as by a pedagogue, they might be led by the hand to the point where they might hear the things He commands, according to the words given below: **the law was our pedagogue in Christ, that we might be justified by faith** (3:24). But after we have access to the Father through Christ, as is said in Romans (5:2), we are not instructed about the commands of God through the Law, but by God Himself. Hence he says: Through the Law leading me by the hand I have died to the written law, in order that I may live unto God, i.e., to the maker of the Law, i.e., to be instructed and directed by Him.

Then when he says, **with Christ I am nailed to the cross,** he amplifies what he said. Now he had said that he died to the Law and lives unto God. Hence he explains these two things:

> First, that he died to the Law, he explains by saying that **with Christ I am nailed to the cross;**
> Secondly, that he lives unto God, when he says (v. 20): **I live, now not I, but Christ liveth in me.**

The first point can be explained in two ways. In one way, as in a Gloss, thus: every man according to carnal origin is born a child of wrath: "By nature we were children of wrath, even as the rest" (Eph. 2:3). He is also born in the oldness of sin: "Thou art grown old in a strange country" (Bar. 3:11).

This oldness of sin is removed by the cross of Christ, and the newness of spiritual life is conferred. Therefore the Apostle says, **with Christ I am nailed to the cross,** i.e., concupiscence or the inclination to sin, and all such have been put to death in me through the cross of Christ: "Our old man is crucified with him, that the body of sin may be destroyed" (Rom. 6:6). Also from the fact that I am crucified with Christ and have died to sin; and because Christ rose again, I, too, have risen with Him rising: "Who was delivered up for our sins, and rose again for our justification" (Rom. 4:25). Thus, therefore, does Christ beget a new life in us, after the oldness of sin has been destroyed. Hence he says, **And I live,** i.e., because I am nailed to the cross of Christ, I have the strength to act well, **now not I** according to the flesh, because I no longer have the oldness which I formerly had, **but Christ liveth in me,** i.e., the newness which has been given to us through Christ.

Or, in another way: a man is said to live according to that in which he chiefly puts his affection and in which he is mainly delighted. Hence men who take their greatest pleasure in study or in hunting say that this is their life. However, each man has his own private interest by which he seeks that which is his own. Therefore, when someone lives seeking only what is his own, he lives only unto himself; but when he seeks the good of others, he is said to live for them. Accordingly, because the Apostle had set aside his love of self through the cross of Christ, he said that he was dead so far as love of self was concerned, declaring that **with Christ I am nailed to the cross,** i.e., through the cross of Christ my own private love has been removed from me. Hence he says **God forbid that I should glory save in the cross of our Lord Jesus Christ** (6:14): "If one died for all, then all were dead. And Christ died for all, that they also who live may not now live to themselves, but unto him who died for them" (2 Cor. 5:14). **And I live, now not I,** i.e., I no longer live as though having any interest in my own good, **but Christ liveth**

**in me,** i.e., I have Christ alone in my affection and Christ Himself is my life: "To me, to live is Christ; and to die is gain" (Phil. 1:21).

Then when he says, **And that I live now in the flesh, I live in the faith of the Son of God,** he answers a twofold difficulty that might arise from his words. One is how he lives and yet it is not he who lives; the second is how he is nailed to the cross. Therefore he clears up these two points. First of all, the first one, namely, how he lives and yet it is not he who lives. He answers this when he says **And that I live now in the flesh, I live in the faith of the Son of God.** Here it should be noted that, strictly speaking, those things are said to live which are moved by an inner principle. Now the soul of Paul was set between his body and God; the body, indeed, was vivified and moved by the soul of Paul, but his soul by Christ. Hence as to the life of the flesh, Paul himself lived and this is what he says, namely, **and that I live now in the flesh,** i.e., by the life of the flesh; but as to his relation to God, Christ lived in Paul. Therefore he says, **I live in the faith of the Son of God** through which He dwells in me and moves me: "But the just shall live in his faith" (Hab. 2:4). And note that he says **in the flesh,** not "by the flesh," because this is evil.

Secondly, he shows that he is nailed to the cross, saying: Because the love of Christ, which He showed to me in dying on the cross for me, brings it about that I am always nailed with Him. And this is what he says, **who loved me:** "He first loved us" (1 Jn. 4:10). And He loved me to the extent of **giving himself** and not some other sacrifice **for me:** "He loved us and washed us from our sins in his own blood" (Apoc. 1:5); "As Christ loved the church and delivered himself up for it, that he might sanctify it, cleansing it by the laver of water in the word of life" (Eph. 5:25).

But it should be noted that the Son delivered Himself, and the Father His Son: "He spared not even his own Son, but delivered him up for us" (Rom. 8:32). Judas, too, delivered Him up, as is said in Matthew (26:48). It is all one event, but the intention is not the same, because the Father did so out of love, the Son out of obedience along with love, but Judas out of avarice and treachery.

Then when he says, **I cast not away the grace of God,** he draws the principal conclusion. First, he draws the conclusion; secondly, he explains it. He says, therefore: Because I have received from God so great a grace that He delivered Himself, and I live in the faith of the Son of God, **I cast not away the grace of God,** i.e., I do not repudiate it or show myself ungrateful: "The grace of God in me hath not been void, but I have labored more abundantly than all they" (1 Cor. 15:10). Hence another version has, "I am not ungrateful for the grace of God." "Looking diligently lest any man be wanting to the grace of God" (Heb. 12:15), i.e., by showing myself unworthy because of ingratitude.

A form of repudiation and of ingratitude would exist, if I were to say that the Law is necessary in order to be justified. Hence he says, **For if justice be by the law, then Christ died in vain,** i.e., if the Law is sufficient, i.e., if the works of the Law suffice to justify a man, Christ died to no purpose and in vain, because He died in order to make us just: "Christ also died once for our sins, the just for the unjust, that he might offer us to God" (1 Pet. 3:18). Now if this could have been done through the Law, the death of Christ would have been superfluous. But He did not die in vain or labor to no purpose, as it is said in Isaias (49:4); because through Him alone came justifying grace and truth, as it is said in John (1:17). Therefore, if any were just before the passion of Christ, this too was through the faith of Christ to come, in Whom they believed and in Whose faith they were saved.

# CHAPTER 3

## LECTURE 1

1 O senseless Galatians, who hath bewitched you that you should not obey the truth; before whose eyes Jesus Christ hath been set forth, crucified among you?

Above, the Apostle reproved the Galatians for their vanity and fickleness on the authority of the Gospel teaching by showing that his doctrine was approved by the other apostles. Now through reason and authority he proves the same thing, namely, that the works of the Law must not be observed. This he does in two ways:

First, from the insufficiency of the Law;
Secondly, from the dignity of those who have been converted to Christ (4:1).

Concerning the first he does two things:

First, he utters the rebuke;
Secondly, he begins his proof (v. 2).

As to the first, he does two things:

First, he rebukes them by showing that they are foolish;
Secondly, he gives the reason for his rebuke (v. 1): **before whose eyes Jesus Christ hath been set forth.**

First, therefore, he chides them for their folly, calling them senseless. Hence he says, **O senseless Galatians.** Now "senseless" is properly said of one who lacks sense. But the spiritual sense is knowledge of the truth. Hence anyone who lacks the truth is appropriately called senseless: "Are you also yet without understanding?" (Mt. 15:16); "We fools esteemed their life madness" (Wis. 5:4).

But against this, it is said in Matthew (5:22): "Whosoever shall say to his brother, Thou fool, shall be in danger of hell-fire." Now a fool is the same as senseless. Therefore, the Apostle was in danger of hell-fire. But it must be said, as Augustine suggests, that this applies if it is said without reason and with the intention to disparage. But the Apostle said it with reason and with an intention to correct. Hence a Gloss says: "He says this in sorrow."

Secondly, when he says, **who hath bewitched you that you should not obey the truth,** he shows how they had become senseless. Here it is to be noted, first of all, that someone becomes senseless in a number of ways: either because some truth he could know is not proposed to him; or because he departs from a truth that had been proposed and accepted, as when he abandons the way of truth. Such were these Galatians who rejected the truth proposed to them and abandoned the truth of the faith they had accepted: **I wonder that you are so soon removed from him that called you into the grace of Christ, unto another gospel** (1:6). This, therefore, is the type of senselessness for which he chides them when he says: **who hath bewitched you that you should not obey the truth?**

To understand what bewitchment is, it should be noted that according to a Gloss, bewitchment is, properly speaking, a sense delusion usually produced by magical arts; for example, to make a man appear to onlookers as a lion or as having horns. This can also be brought about by demons who have the power to set phantasms in motion as well as to produce in the senses the very alterations that real objects are wont to produce. According to this acceptation the Apostle asks, appropriately enough, **who hath bewitched you?** As if to say: You are as deluded men who take obvious things to be other than they are in very fact, namely, because you are deluded by artifices and sophisms, **not to obey**

**the truth,** i.e., you neither see the obvious truth received by you nor embrace it by obeying it: "For the bewitching of vanity obscureth good things" (Wis. 4:12); "Woe to you that call evil good, and good evil" (Is. 5:20). In another way bewitchment is taken to mean that someone is harmed by an evil look, particularly when cast by sorcerers whose inflamed eyes and hostile glance cast a spell on boys who grow faint from it and vomit their food.

Avicenna, attempting to explain this phenomenon in his book *On the Soul,* says that corporeal matter obeys an intellectual substance more than it obeys the active and passive qualities at work in nature. Accordingly, he supposes that through the mental activity of intellectual substance (which he calls the souls or movers of the heavenly spheres) many things occur outside the order of heavenly movements and of all corporeal forces. Along the same lines he says that when a holy soul is purged of all earthly affection and carnal vice, it acquires a likeness to the aforesaid substances, so that nature obeys it. This is why certain holy men achieve marvels that transcend the course of nature. In like manner, because the soul of someone defiled by carnal passions has a vigorous apprehension of malice, nature obeys it to the point of affecting matter, particularly in those in whom the matter is pliant, as in the case of tender children. Thus does it happen, according to him, that from the vigorous apprehension exercised by sorcerers a child can be evilly affected and bewitched. This position seems to be true enough according to Avicenna's tenets. For he postulates that all material forms in sublunar bodies are influenced by the separated incorporeal substances and that natural agents can be no more than dispositive causes in such matter.

However, this is disproved by the Philosopher. For an agent should be similar to what is subject to it. Now what comes into existence is not a form alone or matter alone but the composite of matter and form. Consequently, that which acts to produce the existence of corporeal things ought to have matter and form. Therefore he says that the only thing which can cause changes of matter and form is something that itself has matter and form either virtually, as God, who is the maker of form and matter, or actually, as a bodily agent. Therefore with respect to forms of this kind corporeal matter obeys the nod neither of angels nor of any mere creature but of God alone, as Augustine says. Hence what Avicenna says about this matter of bewitchment is not true.

Therefore it is better to say that when a man's act of imagining or apprehending is strong, the sense is affected or at least the sense appetite is. Now such as affection does not occur without some alteration taking place in the body and the bodily spirits; as, for example, we see that when something pleasant is apprehended, the sense appetite is moved to desire and as a result the body becomes warm. Similarly, as a result of apprehending something horrible, the body grows cold. When the spirits are thus moved they mainly infect the eyes, which in turn infect certain things through their glance, as is plain in the case of a clean mirror that becomes defiled when looked into by a woman in her monthly purification. Therefore because sorcerers are obstinate and hardened in evil, their sense appetite is affected by the vigor of their apprehension; as a result, as has been said, the infection moves from the veins to the eyes and thence to the object upon which they look. Accordingly, because the flesh of children is soft, it is influenced and charmed by their hostile glance. And demons, too, can sometimes produce this effect.

He says, therefore, **who hath bewitched you that you should not obey the truth?** As if to say: You once obeyed the truth of the faith, but now you do not. Therefore, you are as children infected by some hostile glance who vomit the food they have eaten.

Then he tells why he rebukes them, when he says, **before whose eyes Jesus Christ hath been set forth, crucified among you.** This can be interpreted in three ways. One way, Jerome's, corresponds to the first meaning of "bewitchment"; as if he

says: I say that you are bewitched, because **before your eyes
Christ hath been set forth,** i.e., the outlawing of Christ, Who
was condemned to death, is as vivid to your eyes as if it were
being enacted before your eyes and He was being crucified
among you, i.e., the crucifixtion of Christ was as clear in your
understanding as though it were taking place there. Hence, if
you no longer see it, it is because you have been deluded and
bewitched. Against such a change of heart, it is said in the
Canticle (8:6): "Put me as a seal upon thy heart, as a seal upon
thy arm."

Another way, Augustine's, is as if he said: You are justifi-
ably bewitched, because as children, you vomit out the truth
you have received, namely, Christ by faith in your hearts. And
you do this because **before your eyes,** i.e., in your presence,
**Jesus Christ is outlawed,** i.e., expelled and refused His inheritance. This should trouble you, because the very one whom you
should not allow to be outlawed and expelled by others has
been outlawed among you, i.e., has lost His inheritance,
namely, yourselves, among you. Then that which follows,
namely, **crucified,** should be read "with a heavy burden and
obvious pain," because he adds this to make them consider the
great price Christ paid for the inheritance He lost among them,
and thus move them more deeply. As if to say: Christ has been
outlawed among you, He Who was crucified, i.e., Who with
His cross and His own blood purchased this inheritance: "You
are bought with a great price" (1 Cor. 6:20); "Knowing that
you were not redeemed with corruptible things, as gold or
silver, from your vain conversation of the tradition of your
fathers; but with the precious blood of Christ, as of a lamb
unspotted and undefiled" (1 Pet. 1:18).

The third way, Ambrose's, is as though he says: Yes, you
are bewitched, you, **before whose eyes,** i.e., in whose opinion,
namely, according to your judgment, **Jesus Christ is outlawed,**
i.e., condemned without saving others. **And among you,** i.e., so
far as you understand, **He was crucified,** i.e., merely died, but
justified no one in spite of the fact that it is said of Him, "Al-

though he was crucified through weakness, yet he liveth by the power of God" (2 Cor. 13:4).

It can be explained also in a fourth way according to a Gloss to the effect that by these words the Apostle proclaims the gravity of their guilt, because in deserting Christ by observing the Law, they sin somewhat on a par with Pilate who outlawed Christ, i.e., condemned him. For in believing that Christ does not suffice to save them, they are made to be sinners similar to Christ's executioners who hung Him on the cross, condemning Him to a most shameful death and killing Him. The parity is taken on the side of the one against whom they sinned, because the Galatians sinned against Christ Jesus as did Pilate and those who crucified Christ.

# CHAPTER 3

## LECTURE 2

2 This only would I learn of you: Did you receive the Spirit by the works of the law or by the hearing of faith?

3 Are you so foolish that, whereas you began in the Spirit, you would now be made perfect by the flesh?

4 Have you suffered so great things in vain? If it be yet in vain.

5 He, therefore, who giveth to you the Spirit and worketh miracles among you; doth he do it by the works of the law or by the hearing of the faith?

Having given his rebuke, the Apostle goes on to show the insufficiency of the Law, and the power of the faith.

First, he proves the insufficiency of the Law;
Secondly, he raises a question and answers it (v. 19).

Concerning the first, he does two things:

First, he proves the deficiency and insufficiency of the Law by appealing to what they experienced;
Secondly, by authority and reasons (v. 6).

As to the first, he does two things:

First, he proves his proposition by appealing to something
   they experienced;
Secondly, by using something he himself experienced
   (v. 5).

With respect to the first, he does two things:

First, he discusses the gift they have received;
Secondly, the defect into which they have fallen (v. 3).

He discusses the gift they received by asking them from
whom they received it. Hence, presupposing that they accepted the gift, he interrogates them and asks: Although you
have been bewitched and are foolish, nevertheless you are not
so deluded that you cannot explain to me something very obvious. Hence he says, **This only would I learn of you,** because
this by itself is enough to prove my point; namely, it is evident
that you have received the Holy Spirit. I ask, therefore, **Did
you receive the Spirit by the works of the law or by the hearing
of faith?**

To elucidate this, it should be noted that in the early
Church, by God's providence, in order that the faith of Christ
might prosper and grow, manifest signs of the Holy Spirit took
place in the hearers immediately after the apostles preached
the faith. Accordingly, it is said of Peter in Acts (10:44):
"While Peter was yet speaking these words, the Holy Spirit
fell on all them that heard the word." The Galatians, too,
openly received the Holy Spirit at Paul's preaching. The Apostle therefore asks them: Whence did they obtain the Holy
Spirit? For it is obvious that it was not through the works of
the Law, because, since they were Gentiles, they did not have
the Law before they received the Holy Spirit. Therefore they
had the Holy Spirit, i.e., the gifts of the Holy Spirit, by the
hearing of faith: "For you have not received the spirit of bondage again in fear," which was given in the Law (for the Law
was given amid tremors), "but you have received the spirit of
adoption of sons," (Rom. 8:17). Therefore, if the power of the

faith could do this, it is vain to seek something else by which
we are saved, because it is more difficult to make the unjust
just than to preserve the just in their justice. Hence if the faith
had made the unjust Gentiles just without the Law, no doubt
it could without the Law keep them just. Great, therefore,
was the gift they had received through faith.

Then when he says, **Are you so foolish that, whereas you
began in the Spirit, you would now be made perfect by the
flesh?** he shows the defect into which they have fallen. And he
amplifies a twofold defect, touching, namely, the gifts they had
received from Christ and the evils they endured for Him
(v. 4): **Have you suffered so great things in vain?**

Concerning the first, it should be noted that the Galatians,
after they left what was great, namely, the Holy Spirit, ad-
hered to something less, namely, the carnal observances of the
Law—and this is foolish. Hence he says, **Are you so foolish
that, whereas you began** under the inspiration of **the Holy
Spirit,** i.e., obtained the beginning of your perfection from the
Holy Spirit, **you would now,** while you are more perfect, **be
made perfect by the flesh,** i.e., do you seek to be preserved by
the carnal observances of the Law from which you could acquire not even the beginning of justice? "The flesh profiteth
nothing" (Jn. 6:64). Thus do you pervert right order, because
the path of perfection consists in going from the imperfect to
the perfect. But you, because you are doing the opposite, are
foolish: "A holy man continueth in wisdom as the sun; but a
fool is changed as the moon" (Ecclus. 27:12). They are as those
who begin to serve God with fervor of spirit but afterwards
desert to the flesh. Again, they are as Nabuchodonosor's statue
with head of gold and feet of clay (Dan. 11:32). Hence it is
said: "They who are in the flesh cannot please God" (Rom.
8:8); **he that soweth in his flesh, of the flesh also shall reap
corruption** (6:8).

Then when he says, **Have you suffered so great things in
vain?** he amplifies their desertion by considering the evils they
endured for Christ. For anyone who receives something with-

out labor does not guard it as something precious; but that
which is obtained by great effort, it is foolish to esteem lightly
and not guard it. Now it was with labor and tribulation suffered
at the hands of their fellow citizens that they had received the
Holy Spirit. That is why he says, **Have you suffered so great
things in vain?** As if to say: You ought not to despise so great
a gift received with labor; **else you have received it in vain,**
i.e., to no purpose, because you endured these things in order
to attain to eternal life: "Tribulation worketh patience, and
patience trial, and trial hope; and hope confoundeth not"
(Rom. 5:3). Hence, if you shut yourselves out from the door to
eternal life by deserting the faith and seeking to be preserved
by carnal observances, it is **in vain,** i.e., uselessly, that **you have
suffered.** And I say, **If it be yet in vain.** He says this because
it was still in their power to repent, if they willed, as long as
they were alive. This shows that certain deadened works are
revived: "Their labors are without fruit, and their works unprofitable" (Wis. 3:11); **I am afraid lest perhaps I have labored in vain among you** (4:11). If this is applied to evil men
who do not repent, it can be said that they suffered without
cause, i.e., a cause that can confer eternal life.

Then when he says, **He, therefore, who giveth to you the
Spirit and worketh miracles among you; doth he do it by the
works of the law or by the hearing of the faith?** he proves his
proposition by appealing to his own experience. For they
might say that although it is true that we received the Holy
Spirit by the hearing of faith, nevertheless it was because of
the devotion he had to the Law that we received the faith he
preached. Hence he says: But even considering the matter not
from your side but from what I have done in giving you
through my ministration the Holy Spirit Who **worketh miracles among you,** do I do this **by the works of the law or by the
hearing of the faith?** In truth, not by the works of the Law but
by faith.

But can anyone give the Holy Spirit? For Augustine in
*On The Trinity* (Bk. XV) says that no mere man can give the

Holy Spirit, for the apostles did not give the Holy Spirit but imposed hands on men, who then received the Holy Spirit. What then does the Apostle mean when he speaks of himself as **giving to you the Holy Spirit?** I answer that in the giving of the Holy Spirit three things conspire in a certain order, namely, the indwelling Holy Spirit, the gift of grace and charity along with the other habits, and the sacrament of the New Law by whose administering He is given. Hence He can be given by someone in three ways.

For He can be given by someone as having authority with respect to all three, namely, in respect to the Holy Spirit's indwelling, in respect to the gift, and in respect to the sacrament. And in this way the Holy Spirit is given by the Father and Son alone, inasmuch as they have the authority not of dominion but of origin, because He proceeds from both.

But as to the grace or gift and as to the sacraments, the Holy Spirit even gives Himself in the sense that the giving implies the causality of the Holy Spirit with respect to His gifts, because, as the Apostle says in 1 Corinthians (12:11): "He divides to everyone according as He wills." But as far as the author of the giving is concerned, it is not appropriate to say that the Holy Spirit gives Himself.

But concerning the sacrament which is given by the ministry of the Church's ministers, it can be said that holy men by administering the sacraments give the Holy Spirit. And this is the way the Apostle had in mind—the way mentioned in a Gloss. Nevertheless, this is not the usual way of putting it, and it ought not be exaggerated.

Again, a Gloss says that the performing of miracles is attributed to faith, which, because it believes in things that are above nature, operates above nature. Hence because the apostles preached the faith which contained things above reason, they should have adduced in support of their credibility some testimony that they had been sent by God—a fact which surpasses reason. Hence Christ gave them His own sign to prove this.

Now there is a twofold sign of Christ. One is that He is the Lord of all; hence it is said: "Thy kingdom is a kingdom of all ages: and thy dominion endureth throughout all generations" (Ps. 144:13). The other is that He is Sanctifier and Savior, according to Acts (4:12): "There is no other name under heaven given to men, whereby we must be saved." Accordingly, He gave them two signs: one was the power to perform miracles, so that they could show they were sent by God, the Lord of all creatures: "He gave them power and authority over all devils and to cure diseases" (Lk. 9:1). The other was that by their ministry they might give the Holy Spirit, in order to show that they had been sent by the Savior of all: "They laid their hands upon them, and they received the Holy Spirit" (Ac. 8:17). Of these two ways it is said in Hebrews (2:4): "God also bearing them witness by signs and wonders and divers miracles and distributions of the Holy Spirit, according to his own will."

# CHAPTER 3

## LECTURE 3

6 As it is written: Abraham believed God; and it was reputed to him unto justice.

7 Know ye, therefore, that they who are of faith, the same are the children of Abraham.

8 And the scripture, foreseeing that God justifieth the Gentiles by faith, told unto Abraham before: In thee shall all nations be blessed.

9 Therefore, they that are of faith shall be blessed with faithful Abraham.

Having proved by experience the power of the faith and the insufficiency of the Law, the Apostle now proves the same things by authority and by reasons.

First, he proves the power of the faith to justify;
Secondly, in this he proves the insufficiency of the Law (v. 10).

The first he proves by using a syllogism. Hence with respect to this he does three things:

First, he proves the minor premise;
Secondly, the major premise (v. 8);
Thirdly, he draws the conclusion (v. 9).

Concerning the first, he does two things:

First, he proposes a certain authority from which he takes the minor;
Secondly, he concludes the minor (v. 7).

He says therefore: Truly, justice and the Holy Spirit come from faith, **As it is written** in Genesis (15:6) and mentioned again in Romans (4:3): **Abraham believed God and it was reputed to him unto justice.** Here it should be noted that justice consists in paying a debt. Now man is indebted to God and to himself and to his neighbor. But it is on account of God that he owes something to himself and his neighbor. Therefore the highest form of justice is to render to God what is God's. For if you render to yourself or your neighbor what you owe and do not do this for the sake of God, you are more perverse than just, since you are putting your end in man. Now, whatever is in man is from God, namely, intellect and will and the body itself, albeit according to a certain order; because the lower is ordained to the higher, and external things to internal, namely, to the good of the soul. Furthermore, the highest thing in man is his mind. Therefore the first element of justice in a man is that a man's mind be subjected to God, and this is done by faith: "Bringing into captivity every understanding unto the obedience of Christ" (2 Cor. 10:5).

Therefore in all things it must be said that God is the first principle in justice and that whosoever gives to God, namely, the greatest thing that lies in him by submitting the mind to Him, such a one is fully just: "Whosoever are led by the Spirit of God, they are the sons of God" (Rom. 8:14). And hence he says, **Abraham believed God,** i.e., submitted his mind to God by faith: "Believe God, and he will recover thee: and direct thy way, and trust in him" (Ecclus. 2:6); and further on (2:8): "Ye that fear the Lord believe him," **and it was reputed to him unto justice,** i.e., the act of faith and faith itself were for him, as for everyone else, the sufficient cause of justice. It is reputed to him unto justice by men exteriorly, but interiorly it is wrought by God, Who justifies them that have the faith. This he does by remitting their sins through charity working in them.

From this authority he draws the minor proposition, saying **Know ye therefore, that they who are of faith, the same are the children of Abraham.** As if to say: Someone is called the son of another because he imitates his works; therefore, "if you be the children of Abraham, do the works of Abraham" (Jn. 8:39). But Abraham did not seek to be justified through circumcision but through faith. Therefore the sons of Abraham are they who seek to be justified by faith. And this is what he says: Because Abraham is just through faith, in that he believed God and it was reputed to him unto justice; **therefore, know ye that they who are of faith,** i.e., who believe that they are justified and saved by faith, **the same are the children of Abraham,** namely, by imitation and instruction: "They that are the children of the promise are accounted for the seed" (Rom. 9:8); "This day is salvation come to this house, because he also is the son of Abraham" (Lk. 19:9); "God is able of these stones," i.e., of the Gentiles, "to raise up children to Abraham," inasmuch as He makes them believers (Mt. 3:9).

Then when he says, **the scripture, foreseeing that God justifieth the Gentiles by faith,** he sets down the major premise, namely, that Abraham was told beforehand that in his seed all nations would be blessed. Hence when he says, **the scripture foreseeing,** he introduces God speaking to Abraham (Gen. 12:3). Therefore he says, **God told unto Abraham before** that **in thee,** i.e., in those who in your likeness will be your sons by imitating your faith, **shall all nations be blessed:** "Many will come from the east and from the west, and shall sit down with Abraham, and Isaac, and Jacob in the kingdom of heaven" (Mt. 8:11).

Then when he says, **Therefore, they that are of faith,** he draws the conclusion from the premises. Accordingly, the argument can be formulated thus: God the Father announced to Abraham that in his seed all nations would be blessed. But those who seek to be justified by faith are the children of Abraham. Therefore, they that are of faith, i.e., who seek to be justified through faith, **shall be blessed with faithful,** i.e., with believing, **Abraham.**

# CHAPTER 3

### LECTURE 4

10 For as many as are of the works of the law are under a curse. For it is written: Cursed is every one that abideth not in all things which are written in the book of the law to do them.

11 But, that in the law no man is justified with God, it is manifest; because the just man liveth in faith.

12 But the law is not of faith; but: he that doth those things shall live in them.

Above, the Apostle proved the power of faith; now he shows the shortcoming of the Law.

First, through the authority of the Law;
Secondly, through a human custom (v. 15).

Concerning the first, he does three things:

First, he shows the curse brought on by the Law;
Secondly, the Law's inability to remove that curse (v. 11);
Thirdly, the sufficiency of Christ by whom that curse has been removed (v. 13).

In regard to the first he does two things:

First, he sets forth his intended proposition;

Secondly, he proves the proposition (v. 10); **For it is written: Cursed is every one that abideth not in all things, which are written in the book of the law to do them.**

He says therefore: **For as many as are of the works of the law, are under a curse.** For since he had said that they who are of faith will be blessed through being sons of Abraham, someone might say that they are blessed both on account of the works of the Law and on account of faith. Hence to exclude this he says: **As many as are of the works of the law are under a curse.**

But against this it can be said that the ancient fathers were of the works of the Law. Therefore they are under a curse and, consequently, damned—which is a Manichean error. Hence it is necessary to understand this correctly. And it should be noted that the Apostle does not say, "As many as observe the works of the Law are under a curse," because this is false when applied to the time of the Law. He says rather: **As many as are of the works of the Law,** i.e., whosoever trust in the works of the Law and believe that they are made just by them **are under a curse.** For it is one thing to be of the works of the Law and another to observe the Law. The latter consists in fulfilling the Law, so that one who fulfills it is not under a curse. But to be of the works of the Law is to trust in them and place one's hope in them. And they that are of the Law in this way **are under a curse,** namely, of transgression; not that the Law produces the curse, for concupiscence does not come from the Law, but the knowledge of sin does, to which we are prone through concupiscence banned by the Law. Therefore, inasmuch as the Law begets a knowledge of sin and offers no help against sin, they are said to be under a curse, since they are powerless to escape it by those works.

Furthermore, some works of the Law are ceremonies carried out in the observances; others are works that pertain to

morals, with which the moral precepts deal. Hence, according
to a Gloss, that which is said here, namely, **as many as are of
the works of the law, are under a curse,** is to be understood of
ceremonial works and not of moral works. Or it should be said
that the Apostle is speaking here of all works, both ceremonial
and moral. For the works are not the cause making one to be
just before God; rather they are the carrying out and manifestation of justice. For no one is made just before God by works
but by the habit of faith, not acquired but infused. And therefore, as many as seek to be justified by works are under a
curse, because sin is not removed nor anyone justified in the
sight of God by them, but by the habit of faith vivified by
charity: "And all these being approved by the testimony of
faith, received not the promise" (Heb. 11:39).

Then when he says, **For it is written: Cursed is every one,
that abideth not in all things, which are written in the book of
the law to do them,** he proves the proposition which, according
to a Gloss, is proved by the fact that no one can keep the Law
in the way in which the Law prescribed: "As many as do not
keep and do all that is written in the book of the law," i.e., who
do not fulfill the whole Law, "cursed shall they be" (Deut.
28:15). But it is impossible to fulfill the whole Law, as it is
said in the Acts (15:10): "Why tempt you God to put a yoke
upon the necks of the disciples which neither our fathers nor
we have been able to bear?" Therefore by the works of the
Law no one is anything but cursed.

In another way the passage, **For it is written . . . ,** can
be taken not as a proof of the proposition but as an exposition
of the proof. As if to say: I say that they are under a curse,
i.e., under that one of which the Law says, **For it is written:
Cursed is every one, that abideth not in all things, which are
written in the book of the law to do them,** where the curse is
understood to refer to sin. For the Law commands that good
be done and evils avoided, and by commanding it puts one
under the obligation without giving the virtue to obey. And
hence he says, **Cursed,** as though placed in contact with evil,

is every one, without exception; because, as it is said in the
Acts (10:34): "God is not a respecter of persons"; that abideth
not to the end: "He that shall persevere to the end" (Mt.
24:13); in all things, not in some only, because as it is said in
James (2:10): "Whosoever shall keep the whole law, but offend
in one point, is become guilty of all"; which are written in the
book of the law to do them, not only to believe or will but actually to fulfill them in their works: "A good understanding to
all that do it" (Ps. 110:10). Yet the holy patriarchs, although
they were of the works of the Law, were nevertheless saved by
faith in one to come, by trusting in His grace and by fulfilling
the Law at least spiritually. "For Moses," says a Gloss, "did
indeed command many things which no one could fulfill, in
order to tame the pride of the Jews who said: 'There are many
willing and able, but no one to command'."

But a difficulty arises about saying Cursed is every one
that abideth not in all things, which are written in the book of
the law to do them. For it is said: "Bless, and curse not" (Rom.
12:14). I answer that to curse is nothing else but to say evil. I
can therefore say that good is evil and evil good, and again,
that good is good and evil evil. The first is what the Apostle
forbids when he says, "Curse not," i.e., do not say that good is
evil and evil good. But the second is lawful. Hence when we
denounce sin, we do indeed curse, not by way of calling good
evil but by saying that evil is evil. Therefore it is lawful to
curse a sinner, i.e., to say that he is addicted to evil or is
evil.

Then when he says, But that in the law no man is justified
with God, it is manifest, he shows the inability of the Law to
snatch us from that curse, for it could not make one just. To
show this he makes use of a syllogism in the second figure.
Justice is by faith, but the Law is not by faith. Therefore the
Law cannot justify. With respect to this, therefore:

> First, he states the conclusion when he says, But that in
> the law no one is justified;

Secondly, the major premiss (v. 11): **because the just man lives by faith;**
Thirdly, the minor (v. 12).

Therefore he says: I say that by the Law a curse was introduced, and yet the Law cannot extricate one from that curse, because it is obvious that no one is justified before God by the Law, i.e., through the works of the Law. On this point it should be noted that those who rejected the Old Testament took occasion to do so from this word. Hence it must be said that no one is justified in the Law, i.e., through the Law. For through it came the knowledge of sin, as is said in Romans (3:20); but justification came not through it: "By the works of the law no flesh shall be justified" (Rom. 3:20).

But against this, it is said in James (2:21): "Was not Abraham our father justified by works?" I answer that "to be justified" can be taken in two senses: either as referring to the execution and manifestation of justice, and in this way a man is justified, i.e., proved just, by the works performed; or as referring to the infused habit of justice, and in this way one is not justified by works, since the habit of justice by which a man is justified before God is not acquired but infused by the grace of faith. Therefore the Apostle says significantly, **with God,** because the justice which is before God is interior in the heart, whereas the justice which is by works, i.e., which manifests that one is just, is before men. And it is in this sense that the Apostle says, **with God:** "For not the hearers of the law, but the doers are just before God" (Rom. 2:13); "For if Abraham were justified by works, he hath whereof to glory, but not before God" (Rom. 4:2). Thus, therefore, the conclusion of his reasoning is obvious, namely, that the Law can not justify.

Then when he says, **because the just man lives by faith,** he presents the major premiss, which is based on scriptural authority, i.e., Habacuc (2:4) restated in Romans (1:17) and Hebrews (10:38). Apropos of this point it should be noted that in man there is a twofold life; namely, the life of nature and the life of justice. Now the life of nature is from the soul; hence when the soul is separated from the body, the body continues but is dead. But the life of justice is through God dwelling in us by faith. Therefore the first way in which God is in the soul of man is by faith: "He that cometh to God must believe" (Heb. 11:6); "That Christ may dwell by faith in your hearts" (Eph. 3:17). Accordingly, we say that in the soul the first signs of life appear in the works of the vegetal soul, because the vegetal soul is the first to be present in a generated animal, as the Philosopher says. Similarly, because the first principle whereby God exists in us is faith, faith is called the principle of living. And this is what he means when he says, **the just man lives by faith.** Furthermore, this is to be understood of faith acting through love.

The minor premiss is set down at, **But the law is not of faith.**

First, the minor is set down;
Secondly, it is proved (v. 12): **but he that doth those things, shall live in them.**

He says therefore that **the law is not of faith.** But this seems to conflict with the truth that the Law commands one to believe that there is one God, which pertains to faith. Therefore the Law had faith. And that there is one God is stated in Deuteronomy (6:4): "Hear, O Israel, The Lord our God is one Lord."

I answer that he is speaking here about keeping the commandments of the Law insofar as the Law consists of ceremonial precepts and moral precepts. This is the Law that is not of faith. For "faith," as is said in Hebrews (11:1), "is the substance of things to be hoped for, the evidence of things that appear not." Therefore, strictly speaking, he fulfills the command of faith who does not hope to obtain from it anything present and visible, but things invisible and eternal. Therefore, because the Law promised earthly and present things, as it is said: "If you be willing and will hearken to me, you shall eat the good things of the land" (Is. 1:19), it is not of faith but rather of cupidity or fear, especially in regard to those who kept the Law in a carnal manner. Nevertheless, some did live spiritually in the Law; but this was not because of the Law but because of faith in a mediator.

And that the Law is not of faith he proves when he says, **but he that doth those things,** i.e., the works of the Law, **shall live in them,** namely, in the present life, i.e., will be immune from temporal death and will be preserved in the present life. Or again: I say that the **law is not of faith,** and this is obvious, because **he that doth those things, shall live in them.** As if to say: The precepts of the Law are not concerned with what is to be done, even though it proclaims something that must be believed. Therefore its power is not from faith but from works. He proves this on the ground that when the Lord willed to confirm it He did not say, "He that believeth," but "He that doth those things, shall live in them." But the New Law is from faith: "He that believeth and is baptized shall be saved" (Mk. 16:16).

Nevertheless, the Law is something fashioned and produced by faith. That is why the Old Law is compared to the New as the works of nature to the works of the intellect. For certain works of the intellect appear in the works of nature, not as though natural things understand, but because they are moved and ordained to reach their end by an intellect. In like manner, in the Old Law are contained certain things that are of faith: not that the Jews held them precisely as being of faith, but that they held them only as protestations and figures of the faith of Christ, in virtue of Whose faith the just were saved.

# CHAPTER 3

## LECTURE 5

13 Christ hath redeemed us from the curse of the law, being made a curse for us (for it is written: Cursed is every one that hangeth on a tree);

14 That the blessing of Abraham might come on the Gentiles through Christ Jesus; that we may receive the promise of the Spirit by faith.

Having explained the curse brought on by the Law, as well as the Law's incapacity to deliver from sin, he now shows forth Christ's power to set one free from this curse.

First, he shows how through Christ we are set free of that curse;
Secondly, how in addition we receive help from Christ (v. 14).

As to the first, he does three things:

First, he presents the author of the liberation;
Secondly, the manner of liberation (v. 13): **being made a curse for us;**
Thirdly, the testimony of the prophets (v. 13): **for it is written: Cursed is every one that hangeth on a tree.**

He says therefore first: All who observed the works of the Law were under a curse, as has been said, and they could not be delivered by the Law. Hence it was necessary to have someone who should set us free, and that one was Christ. Hence he says, **Christ hath redeemed us from the curse of the law:** "For what the law could not do, in that it was weak through the flesh, God, sending his own Son in the likeness of sinful flesh and of sin, hath condemned sin in the flesh" (Rom. 8:3). **He redeemed, I say, us,** namely, the Jews, with His own Precious Blood: "Thou hast redeemed us in thy blood" (Apoc. 5:9); "Fear not, for I have redeemed thee" (Is. 43:1), **from the curse of the law,** i.e., from guilt and penalty: **that he might redeem them who were under the law** (4:5); "I will redeem them from death" (Os. 13:14).

Then when he says, **being made a curse for us,** he sets forth the manner of the deliverance. Here it should be noted that a curse is that which is said as an evil. Now it is according to two kinds of evil that there can be two kinds of curse, namely, the curse of guilt and the curse of punishment. And with respect to each this passage can be read, namely, **He was made a curse for us.**

First of all with respect to the evil of guilt, for Christ redeemed us from the evil of guilt. Hence, just as in dying He redeemed us from death, so He redeemed us from the evil of guilt by being made a curse, i.e., of guilt: not that there was really any sin in Him—for "He did not sin, neither was guile found in his mouth," as is said in 1 Peter (2:22) —but only according to the opinion of men and particularly the Jews who regarded him as a sinner: "If he were not a malefactor, we would not have delivered him up to thee" (Jn. 18:30). Hence it is said of Him, "Him who knew no sin He hath made sin for us" (2 Cor. 5:21). But he says, **a curse,** and not "accursed," to show that the Jews regarded Him as the worst type of criminal. Hence it is said, "This man is not of God who keepeth not the sabbath," (Jn. 9:16) and "For a good work we stone thee not, but for sin and for blasphemy" (Jn. 10:33). Therefore he says, **being made for us a curse** in the abstract. As though to say: He was made "curse" itself.

Secondly, it is explained with respect to the evil of punishment. For Christ freed us from punishment by enduring our punishment and our death which came upon us from the very curse of sin. Therefore, inasmuch as He en-

dured this curse of sin by dying for us, He is said to have
been made a curse for us. This is similar to what is said in
Romans (8:3): "God sent his own Son in the likeness of
sinful flesh and of sin," i.e., of mortal sin; "Him who knew
no sin," namely, Christ, Who committed no sin, God (namely,
the Father) "had made sin for us," i.e., made Him suffer the
punishment of sin, when, namely, He was offered for our
sins (2 Cor. 5:21).

Then He gives the testimony of Scripture when he says,
**for it is written: "Cursed is every one that hangeth on a
tree."** This is from Deuteronomy (21:23). Here it should be
noted, according to a Gloss, that in Deuteronomy, from
which this passage is taken, our version as well as the
Hebrew version has: "Cursed by God is everyone that hangs
on a tree." However, the phrase "by God" is not found in
the ancient Hebrew volumes. Hence it is believed to have
been added by the Jews after the passion of Christ in order
to defame Him.

But it is possible to expound this authority both with
respect to the evil of punishment and the evil of guilt. Of
the evil of punishment thus: **Cursed is everyone that hangeth
on a tree,** not precisely because he hangs on a tree, but because of the guilt for which he hangs. And in this way Christ
was thought to be cursed, when He hung on the cross, because He was being punished with an extraordinary punishment. And according to this explanation, there is a continuity
with the preceding. For the Lord commanded in Deuteronomy
that anyone who had been hanged should be taken down in
the evening; the reason being that this punishment was more
disgraceful and ignominious than any other. He is saying,
therefore: Truly was He made a curse for us, because the
death of the cross which He endured is tantamount to a
curse—thus explaining the evil of guilt, although it was only
in the minds of the Jews—because it is written: **Cursed is
everyone that hangeth on a tree.** But with respect to the
evil of punishment, **Cursed is everyone that hangeth on a**

tree is explained thus: The punishment itself is a curse, namely, that He should die in this way. Explained in this way, He was truly cursed by God, because God decreed that He endure this punishment in order to set us free.

Then when he says, **that the blessing of Abraham might come on the Gentiles through Christ Jesus,** he touches on the hope which we acquire through Christ in addition to being freed from the curse: "Not as the offence, so also the gift" (Rom. 5:16), but much greater, namely, because He both frees us from sin and confers grace.

First, therefore, he mentions the fruit and those to whom it is given, saying, **that the blessing of Abraham might come on the Gentiles through Christ Jesus.** As if to say: He was made a curse for us not only to remove a curse but also to enable the Gentiles, who were not under the curse of the Law, to receive the blessing promised to Abraham: "In thy seed shall all the nations of the earth be blessed" (Gen. 22:18). And this blessing was made to us, i.e., fulfilled, through Christ, Who is of the seed of Abraham to whom the promises were made **and to thy seed, who is Christ,** as is said below (v. 16). Now this blessing, this fruit, is **that we may receive the promise of the Spirit,** i.e., the promises which the Holy Spirit, given to us as a pledge and an earnest, works in us concerning eternal happiness which He promises to us, as is said in Ephesians (Ch. 1) and in 2 Corinthians (Ch. 6). Furthermore, in the pledge is contained a guarantee, for a pledge is an assured promise concerning something to be received: "For you have not received the spirit of bondage again in fear, but you have received the spirit of adoption of sons" (Rom. 8:15), and, "and if sons, heirs also" (v. 17). Or: **that we may receive the promise of the Spirit,** i.e., the Holy Spirit. As if to say: That we may receive the promise made to the seed of Abraham concerning the Holy Spirit: "Upon my servants I will pour forth my spirit" (Jl. 2:29). For it is through the Spirit that we are joined to Christ and become children of Abraham worthy of the blessing.

Secondly, he shows how this fruit comes to us, saying, **by faith,** through which also we obtain an eternal inheritance: "He that cometh to God must believe that He is, and is a rewarder to them that seek him" (Heb. 11:6). Through faith, too, we receive the Holy Spirit, because as is said in Acts (Ch. 5) the Lord gives the Holy Spirit to those who obey Him, namely, through faith.

# CHAPTER 3

## LECTURE 6

15 Brethren (I speak after the manner of man), yet a man's testament, if it be confirmed, no man despiseth nor addeth to it.

16 To Abraham were the promises made and to his seed. He saith not: And to his seeds, as of many; but as of one: And to thy seed, which is Christ.

17 Now this I say: that the testament which was confirmed by God, the law which was made after four hundred and thirty years doth not disannul, to make the promise of no effect.

18 For, if the inheritance be of the law, it is no more of promise. But God gave it to Abraham by promise.

Having proved by authority that the Law does not justify and is not necessary for justification, which is through faith, the Apostle then proves the same point with human reasons. Concerning this he does four things:

First, he mentions a human custom;
Secondly, he touches on a divine promise (v. 16);
Thirdly, he draws his conclusion (v. 17);
Fourthly, he shows that the conclusion follows from the premisses (v. 18).

He says therefore: It is clear that up to now I have been speaking according to the authority of Sacred Scripture, which came not by the will of man, but by the Holy Spirit, as is said in 2 Peter (1:21). But now **I speak after the manner of man** and after the manners which human reason and human custom follow. Here, indeed, we have an argument to show that in discussions bearing on faith, we may use any truth of any science: "If thou seest in the number of the captives a beautiful woman and lovest her and wilt have her to wife, thou shalt bring her into thy house," i.e., if you are pleased with worldly wisdom and science, bring it within your boundaries, "and she shall shave her hair, and pare her nails," i.e., you shall cut away all erroneous opinions (Deut. 21:11). This is why in many places in his epistles the Apostle uses the authority of the Gentiles; for example: "Evil communications corrupt good manners" (1 Cor. 15:33), and "The Cretans are always liars, evil beasts, slothful bellies" (Tit. 1:12).

Or: although such reasons be fruitless and weak, because, as is said in Psalm 93 (v. 11): "The Lord knoweth the thoughts of men, that they are vain," yet **a man's testament, if it be confirmed, no one despiseth nor addeth to it,** because nothing human has as much power to bind as a man's last will. But someone would be scorning it if he were to say that a man's will, confirmed by his death and by witnesses, had no validity. Therefore, if no one scorns a testament of this kind by saying that it should not be heeded or by modifying it, much less may anyone scorn the testament of God or modify it and weaken it by adding or removing anything: "If any man shall add to these things, God shall add unto him the plagues written in this book: and if any man shall take away from the words of the book of this prophecy, God shall take away his part out of the book of life" (Apoc. 22:18); "You shall not add to the word that I speak to you, neither shall you take away from it" (Deut. 4:2).

Then when he says, **To Abraham were the promises made,** he takes up the promise God made to Abraham, which is, as it were, the testament of God.

First, he explains this promise or testament;
Secondly, he discloses the truth contained therein (v. 16):
**He saith not: And to his seeds.**

He says therefore: **To Abraham were the promises made.**
As if to say: As the testament of a man is valid, so the divine
promises are valid. But did God make any promises before
the Law? He did; because **To Abraham** who lived before the
time of the Law **the promises were spoken,** i.e., made, **and
to his seed,** by God. However, they were made to Abraham
as the one for whom they would be fulfilled, and to his seed
as the one through whom they would be fulfilled. And he
says, **promises,** using the plural, because the promise that his
seed would be blessed contained a number of things: or because the same thing, namely, eternal happiness, was promised
to him on a number of occasions. For example, "In thee shall
all the kindred of the earth be blessed" (Gen. 12:3); "Look
up to heaven and number the stars if thou canst. So shall
thy seed be" (Gen. 15:5). Again: "To thy seed will I give
this land" (Gen. 15:18); "I will bless thee and I will multiply
thy seed as the stars of heaven" (Gen. 22:17). These promises
then, are God's treatment, as it were, i.e., a decree concerning the inheritance to be given to Abraham and his seed.

The meaning of this testament he explains when he says,
**He saith not: "And to his seeds," as of many; but as of one:
"And to thy seed."** He explains this according to the very
spirit in which the testament was made. And this is obvious
from the words of the testament: **He saith not: "and to his
seeds," as of many,** i.e., as He would do, if it were valid for
many: **but as of one: "And to thy seed," which is Christ,**
because He is the only one through Whom and in Whom
all could be blessed. For He alone and exclusively is the
one who does not lie under the curse of guilt, in spite of
the fact that He deigned to be made a curse for us. Hence
it is said, "I am alone until I pass" (Ps. 140:10); and again
"There is none that doth good, no not one" (Ps. 13:3); "One
man among a thousand I have found" (namely, Christ, Who

had been without any sin), "a woman among them all I have not found," who would be entirely immune from all sin, at least original or venial (Eccl. 7:29).

Then when he says, **Now this I say: that the testament which was confirmed by God,** he draws his conclusion. Here let us see, in order, what it is that he says. He says therefore that this is what God promised to Abraham. But this is a **testament,** i.e., a promise that he would obtain an inheritance: "I will make a new covenant with the house of Israel and with the house of Juda" (Jer. 31:31). He says, **confirmed** (in keeping with what he said above, namely, **a man's testament, if it be confirmed, no man despiseth nor addeth to it**) **by God,** i.e., by the One who promised. **The testament was confirmed,** namely, with an oath: "By my own self have I sworn" (Gen. 22:16); "That by two immutable things in which it is impossible for God to lie, we may have the strongest comfort" (Heb. 6:18). This testament, I say, the Law doth not disannul: **the law,** namely, **which was made** and given by God through Moses: "For the law was given by Moses" (Jn. 1:17) **after four hundred thirty years.** Then, as if to explain what he had said, he adds, **doth not disannul to make the promise of no effect.** For the aforesaid testament would have been disannulled if the promise made to Abraham were set aside, i.e., made fruitless, as though the seed promised to Abraham were not enough to bless the Gentiles. But as a matter of fact, the promises made to the patriarchs were not set aside by Christ but confirmed: "For I say that Christ Jesus was minister of the circumcision to confirm the promises made unto the fathers" (Rom. 15:8); "For all the promises of God are in him 'It is'" (2 Cor. 1:20). **After four hundred thirty years**—this concords with Exodus (12:40): "The abode of the children of Israel that they made in Egypt was four hundred thirty years," and with Acts (7:6): "And God said to him," i.e., to Abraham, "that his seed should sojourn in a strange country and that they shall bring them under bondage four hundred thirty years."

But against this, it is said in Genesis (15:13): "Know thou before that thy seed shall be a stranger in a land not their own, and they shall bring them under bondage and afflict them four hundred years."

I answer that if you count the years between the first promise made to Abraham (Genesis Ch. 12), and the exodus of the children of Israel from Egypt (when the Law was given) there will be four hundred thirty years, as is written here and in Exodus (Ch. 12) and Acts (Ch. 7). But if you begin to count from the birth of Isaac, concerning which Genesis (Ch. 21) speaks, there are only four hundred five years. For twenty-five years elapsed between the promise made to Abraham and the birth of Isaac: for Abraham was seventy-five years old when he left his own country and the first promise was made to him, as is recorded in Ch. 21 of Genesis; and he was one hundred years old when Isaac was born, as is recorded in the same chapter. That there were four hundred five years between the birth of Isaac and the exodus of the children of Israel from Egypt is proved by the fact that Isaac was sixty years old when he begot Jacob, as is had in Genesis (Ch. 25). Jacob, on the other hand, was one hundred thirty years old when he entered Egypt, as is recorded in Genesis (Ch. 47). Therefore from the birth of Isaac to Jacob's entry into Egypt were one hundred ninety years. Now Joseph was thirty years old when he stood before Pharao, as is recorded in Genesis (Ch. 41). After that there were seven years of plenty and two of want; and it was after that that Jacob came to Egypt, as is recorded in Genesis (Ch. 45). But Joseph lived one hundred ten years, as is mentioned in the final chapter of Genesis. If thirty-nine years be subtracted from this there remain seventy-one years. Consequently from the birth of Isaac to Joseph's death there were two hundred sixty-one years. Furthermore, the children of Israel remained in Egypt for one hundred forty-four more years after Joseph's death, as Rabanus says in a Gloss on the Acts (Ch. 7). Therefore from the birth of Isaac to the

exodus from Egypt and the giving of the Law four hundred
five years elapsed. However, the scripture in Genesis (Ch.
17) was not concerned with minutiae. Or it can be said that
during Isaac's fifth year Ismael was cast forth, leaving Isaac
the sole heir of Abraham. Reckoning from this date, we have
our four hundred years.

Then when he says, **For, if the inheritance be of the law,
it is no more of promise,** he shows how from the foregoing
it follows that the Law would nullify the promises, if the
Law were necessary for justification or for the blessing to
come to the Gentiles. He says therefore: The promise would
indeed be disannulled, if the Law were necessary; for **if the
inheritance,** namely, of Abraham's blessing, **be of the law, it
is no more of promise,** i.e., of the seed promised to Abraham.
For if the seed promised to Abraham was enough to obtain
the inheritance of the blessing, there would not be justification through the Law. He rejects the consequent, when he
says, **But God gave it to Abraham,** i.e., He promised that
He would give it; but the promise was as sure as if it had
been fulfilled then and there, **by promise,** i.e., through the
seed promised. Therefore the inheritance, i.e., the blessing
(about which it is said in 1 Peter (3:9): "For unto this are
you called, that you may inherit a blessing") is not of the
Law.

# CHAPTER 3

## LECTURE 7

19 Why then was the law? It was set because of transgressions,
until the seed should come to whom he made the promise, being ordained by angels in the hand of a mediator.
20 Now a mediator is not of one; but God is one.

After showing by the authority of scripture and by a
human custom that the Law was unable to make one just,

the Apostle now raises two questions and solves them. The
second of these begins at (v. 21).

With respect to the first, he does three things:

First, he raises the question;
Secondly, he solves it (v. 19): **It was set because of
transgressions;**
Thirdly, he elucidates something he presupposed in the
course of his solution (v. 20).

The question which might arise from the foregoing is
this: If the Law was unable to justify, was the Law without
purpose? This question he raises when he says, **Why then
was the law?** i.e., what purpose did it serve? This is the
punctuation which, as a Gloss says, Augustine favors, although
earlier he approved the reading, **What then?** followed by,
**The law was set up because of transgressions.** In Romans
(3:1), a similar question is raised: "What advantage then
hath the Jew; or what is the profit of circumcision?"

Then when he says, **It was set because of transgressions,**
he solves the question. Here he does four things:

First, he sets down the purpose of the Law;
Secondly, the fruit of the Law (v. 19); **until the seed
should come to whom he made the promise;**
Thirdly, the ministers of the Law (v. 19): **being ordained by angels;**
Fourthly, the Lord of the Law (v. 19): **in the hand of
a mediator.**

With respect to the first, it should be noted that the
Old Law was given for a fourfold purpose, corresponding to
the four consequences of sin enumerated by Bede, namely,
because of wickedness, weakness, passion, and ignorance.
Hence the Law was given first of all to suppress wickedness,
since by forbidding sin and by punishing, it restrained men
from sin. This he touches on when he says, **The law was
set because of transgressions,** i.e., to prevent them. On this

point it is said: "The law is not made for the just man but for the unjust" (1 Tim. 1:9). The reason for this can be taken from *Ethics IV* of the Philosopher. For men who are well disposed, are inclined to act well of themselves, so that fatherly admonitions are enough for them: hence they do not need a law; indeed, as it is said, "They are a law to themselves who show the work of the law written in their hearts" (Rom. 2:14).

But men who are ill disposed need to be kept from sin by penalties. Hence with respect to such men it was necessary to set down a law which has power to constrain.

Secondly, the Law was set down in order to disclose human weakness. For men gloried in two things: First, in their knowledge; and secondly, in their power. Hence God left men without the instruction of the Law during the period of the Law of nature, during which time, as they fell into errors, their pride was convinced of its lack of knowledge, even though they still presumed on their powers. For they said, "Many are willing and able, but there is no one to lead," as a Gloss says on Exodus (24:8): "All things that the Lord hath spoken we will do. We will be obedient." And therefore the Law was given which would cause a knowledge of sin, "for by the law is the knowledge of sin" (Rom. 3:20). But it did not give the help of grace to avoid sin, so that man, bound by the Law, might test his strength and recognize his infirmity. Finding that without grace he was unable to avoid sin, he would more ardently yearn for grace. And this cause can also be derived from these words, if they are taken to mean that the Law was set for the sake of filling up transgressions, in the sense in which the Apostle speaks when he says: "Now the law entered in that sin might abound" (Rom. 5:20). This is to be taken not in a causal but in a sequential sense; for after the Law entered in, sin abounded and transgressions multiplied, because concupiscence, not yet healed by grace, lusted after that which was forbidden, with the result that sin became more grievous, being now a violation of a written law. But God permitted this in order that men, recognizing their own imperfection, might seek the grace of a mediator. Hence he says significantly, **It was set,** i.e., interposed, as it were, between the Law of nature and the Law of grace.

Thirdly, the Law was given in order to tame the concupiscence of a wanton people, so that, worn out by various ceremonies, they would not fall into idolatry or lewdness. Hence Peter says: "This is a yoke which neither our fathers nor we have been able to bear" (Ac. 15:10).

Fourthly, the Law was given as a figure of future grace in order to instruct the ignorant, according to Hebrews (10:1): "For the law, having a shadow of the good things to come."

Then [he sets forth the fruit of the Law] when he says, **until the seed should come,** i.e., Christ, of Whom God had promised that through Him all nations would be blessed: "For all the prophets and the law prophesied until John" (Mt. 11:13); "In thy seed shall all the nations of the earth be blessed" (Gen. 22:18).

The ministers of the Law are mentioned when he says, **ordained,** i.e., given in good order, **by angels,** i.e., the messengers of God, namely, Moses and Aaron: "They shall seek the law at his mouth: because he is the angel of the Lord of hosts" (Mal. 2:7). Or: **by angels,** i.e., by the ministry of angels: "You have received the law by the disposition of angels" (Ac. 7:53). And it was given by angels, because it was not fitting that it be given by the Son, Who is greater: "For if the word spoken by angels became steadfast . . . how shall we escape if we neglect so great salvation? Which, having begun to be declared by the Lord, was confirmed unto us by them that heard him" (Heb. 2:2). Furthermore, he says **ordained,** because it was given in proper sequence, namely, between the time of the Law of nature (during which men were convinced they could not help themselves) and the time of grace. For before they should receive grace, they had to be convinced by the Law.

The Lord of the Law is Christ; hence he says, **in the hand of a mediator**, i.e., in the power of Christ: "In his right hand a fiery law" (Deut. 33:2); "There is one mediator of God and men, the man Christ Jesus" (1 Tim. 2:5). This mediator was represented by Moses in whose hand the Law was given: "I was the mediator, and stood between the Lord and you at that time" (Deut. 5:5).

Then when he says, **Now a mediator is not of one**, he explains what he meant when he said, **in the hand of a mediator**. This can be explained in three ways. In one way, that a mediator is not of one alone but of two. Hence, since He is the mediator of God and men, it was fitting that He be God and man. For were he purely man or solely God, He would not be a true mediator. Therefore, if He is true God, then since no one is his own mediator, someone might suppose that there are, besides Him, other gods of whom He was the mediator. But this he forestalls when he says that although this **mediator is not of one** only, there are not on that account other gods, **but God is one**, because, although He is distinct in person from God the Father, He is not distinct in nature: "Hear, O Israel: the Lord our God is one Lord" (Deut. 6:4); "One Lord, one faith, one baptism" (Eph. 4:6).

In a second way, because someone might believe that He was the mediator of the Jews alone, he says: I say that Christ is mediator; but not of one, i.e., of the Jews, but one of all, i.e., capable of reconciling everyone to God, because He is God: "For it is one God that justifieth circumcision by faith and uncircumcision through faith" (Rom. 3:30); "For God indeed was in Christ reconciling the world to himself" (2 Cor. 5:19).

In a third way, namely, that He is not a mediator of only one people, namely, the Jews, but of the Gentiles as well: "For he is our peace, who hath made both one" (Eph. 2:14); on the part of the Gentiles by taking away idolatry, and on the part of the Jews by delivering them from the observances of the Law. Specifically it is not the Father, not the Holy Spirit, but the Son who is mediator; nevertheless, God is one.

# CHAPTER 3

## LECTURE 8

21 Was the law then against the promises of God? God forbid! For, if there had been a law given which could give life, verily justice should have been by the law.

22 But the scripture hath concluded all under sin, that the promise, by the faith of Jesus Christ, might be given to them that believe.

23 But, before the faith came, we were kept under the law shut up, unto that faith which was to be revealed.

24 Wherefore the law was our pedagogue in Christ; that we might be justified by faith.

25 But, after the faith is come, we are no longer under a pedagogue.

Here, the Apostle raises the other question, namely, whether the Law is injurious to grace. First, he raises the question, saying, **Was the law then against the promises of God?** As if to say: If the Law was set because of transgressions, does the Law go counter to the promises of God, namely, so that what God promised He would do through the promised seed, He would do through another? **God forbid!** As if to say: No. For earlier he had said: **The law doth not disannul to make the promise of no effect** (3:17); "The law, indeed is holy and the commandment holy" (Rom. 7:12).

Secondly, when he says, **For, if there had been a law given which could give life, verily justice should have been by the law,** he answers the question.

First, he shows that the Law is not contrary to the promises of God;

Secondly, that the Law is in keeping with the promises (v. 22).

He says, therefore, that although the Law was set because of transgressions, nevertheless, it is not contrary to the promise of God in being unable to remove those transgressions. For if it were to remove them, then it would obviously be against the promises of God, because justice would be obtained by means other than God promised, since it would be through the Law and not through faith; whereas it is said: "The just shall live in his faith" (Hab. 2:4); "The justice of God is by faith of Jesus Christ" (Rom. 3:22). Hence he says that **if there had been a law given** such **that it could give life,** i.e., of such power as to confer grace and eternal happiness, then **verily** and not seemingly, **justice should have been by the law,** if the Law were to effect what faith is said to effect. Thus faith would serve no end. But the Law does not give life, because "the letter of the law killeth," as is said in 2 Cor. (3:6); "For the law of the spirit of life, in Christ Jesus, hath delivered me from the law of sin and of death" (Rom. 8:2).

Then when he says, **But the scripture hath concluded all under sin,** he shows that the Law is not only not opposed to grace but serves it.

First, he shows that the Law serves God's promises;
Secondly, how this service was made manifest in the case of the Jews (v. 23);
Thirdly, how the Gentiles even without the Law obtained the promises of God (v. 26).

With respect to the first it should be noted that in general the Law serves the promises of God in two ways. First, because it exposes sin: "For by the law is the knowledge of sin" (Rom. 3:20). Secondly, because it reveals human infirmity, in the sense that man cannot avoid sin without grace which was not given by the Law. And just as these two

things, namely, the knowledge of a disease and the infirmity
of the patient is a great inducement to seek medical treatment, so the knowledge of sin and of one's impotency lead
us to seek Christ. Thus, therefore, is the Law the servant
of grace, inasmuch as it affords a knowledge of sin and ac-
tual experience of one's impotency. Hence he says, **the scripture,** i.e., the written Law, **hath concluded,** i.e., held the
Jews enclosed, **under sin,** i.e., showed them the sins they
committed: "For I had not known concupiscence, if the
Law did not say: Thou shalt not covet" (Rom. 7:7). Again,
**hath concluded,** because with the coming of the Law they
took occasion to sin: "For God hath concluded all in unbelief, that He may have mercy on all" (Rom. 11:32). And
all this in order that they would search for grace. Hence he
says, **so that the promise,** i.e., the promised grace, **might be
given** not only to the Jews, but **to all them that believe,** because that grace was able to free from sin; and this grace is
**by the faith of Jesus Christ.**

Then when he says, **But, before the faith came, we were
kept under the law shut up,** he gives experimental evidence
of this service, as manifested in the case of the Jews.

First, he states how the Jews were benefited;
Secondly, he concludes a corollary (v. 24).

He says therefore: If the scripture, i.e., the written Law,
kept all things shut up under sin, what benefits did the Jews
derive from the Law before faith came by grace? He answers
and says: **We** Jews, before the coming of faith, **were kept
under the law,** inasmuch as it made us avoid idolatry and
many other evils; **we were shut up,** I say, not as free men,
but as servants under fear; and this **under the law,** i.e., under the burden and domination of the Law: "The law hath
dominion over a man as long as it liveth" (Rom. 7:1). And
**we were kept shut up,** i.e., protected, in order that we not
be cut off from life, but be made ready **unto that faith which**

was to be revealed: "My salvation is near to come and my
justice to be revealed" (Is. 56:1). And he says, **to be revealed,** because, since faith surpasses all human ingenuity,
it cannot be acquired by one's own skill, but by revelation
and by the gift of God: "The glory of the Lord shall be
revealed, and all flesh together shall see that the mouth of
the Lord hath spoken" (Is. 40:5). Or, **unto that faith,** which
was to be revealed in the time of grace, but which in olden
times was hidden under many signs. Hence in the time of
Christ the veil of the temple was rent (Mt. 27:51).

Then when he says, **the law was our pedagogue in Christ,**
he draws a corollary:

First, he manifests the Law's functions;
Secondly, when its function ceased (v. 25).

The function of the Law was that of a pedagogue; hence
he says, **the law was our pedagogue in Christ.** For as long
as the heir cannot obtain the benefits of his inheritance,
either because he is too young or because of some other
shortcoming, he is sustained, and guarded by a tutor called
a pedagogue, from *paedos* (boy) and *goge* (a guiding). For
under the Law the just were restrained from evil, as help-
less boys are, through fear of punishment; and they were
led to progress in goodness by the love and promise of temporal goods. Further, the Jews were promised that through
a seed that was to come the blessing of an inheritance would
be obtained, but the time for obtaining that inheritance had
not yet come. Consequently, it was necessary that until the
seed should come, they be kept safe and not do unlawful
things. And this was effected by the Law. And therefore he
says, **Wherefore the law was our pedagogue.** As if to say:
By being kept shut up under the Law, **the law was our pedagogue,** i.e., it guided and preserved us, **in Christ,** i.e., in the
way of Christ. And this was done in order **that we might
be justified by the faith** of Christ: "Israel was a child and I

loved him" (Os. 11:1); "Thou hast chastised me and I was instructed" (Jer. 31:18); "For we account a man to be justified by faith without the works of the law" (Rom. 3:28). And although the Law was our pedagogue, it did not bring us the full inheritance, because as is said in Hebrews (7:19): "The law brought nothing to perfection." But the Law's function ended after faith came. Hence he says, **But, after the faith is come,** namely, of Christ, **we are no longer under a pedagogue,** i.e., under constraint, which is not necessary for those who are free: "When I was a child, I spoke as a child, I understood as a child, I thought as a child, but when I became a man I put away the things of a child" (1 Cor. 13:11); "If then any be in Christ a new creature, the old things are passed away" (2 Cor. 5:17).

# CHAPTER 3

## LECTURE 9

26 For you are all the children of God, by faith in Christ Jesus.
27 For as many of you as have been baptized in Christ have put on Christ.
28 There is neither Jew nor Greek; there is neither bond nor free; there is neither male nor female. For you are all one in Christ Jesus.
29 And, if you be Christ's, then are you the seed of Abraham, heirs according to the promise.

Here the Apostle shows that the Gentiles obtained the fruit of grace without serving the Law, whereas the Jews obtained it by keeping and serving the Law. Concerning this he does three things:

First, he states his proposition;
Secondly, he elucidates it (v. 27);
Thirdly, from this he proceeds to his argument (v. 29).

He says therefore: Verily, we are not under the Law,
i.e., under a pedagogue, or under restraint, because we are
the sons of God. In like manner, you, too, are neither under
the Law nor under a pedagogue; for you have attained to
grace. Hence **you are all the children of God by faith** and
not through the Law: "For you have not received the spirit
of bondage" (i.e., of fear which was given in the Old Law),
"but you have received the spirit of adoption of sons," namely,
of charity and love which is given in the New Law through
faith (Rom. 8:15); "He gave them power to be made the
sons of God, to them that believe in his name" (Jn. 1:12).
If, then, you are the sons of God by faith, why do you wish
to become slaves by the observances of the Law? For faith
alone makes man the adopted son of God. Indeed, no one
is an adopted son unless he is united to and cleaves to the
natural son: "For whom he foreknew, he also predestinated
to be made conformable to the image of his Son; that he
might be the firstborn among many brethren" (Rom. 8:29).
For faith makes us sons in Jesus Christ: "That Christ may
dwell by faith in your hearts" (Eph. 3:17). And this **in
Christ Jesus,** i.e., you are sons of God through Jesus Christ.

Then when he says, **For as many of you as have been
baptized in Christ have put on Christ,** he expounds his proposition. Concerning this he does three things:

> First, he proposes to explain the proposition;
> Secondly, the elucidation of the explanation (v. 28);
> Thirdly, he assigns the reason behind the explanation (v.
> 28): **For you are all one in Christ Jesus.**

With respect to the first, he shows how we are sons of
God in Christ Jesus. And he says: **For as many of you as
have been baptized in Christ have put on Christ.** Now this
can be explained in four ways. In one way, so that **as many
of you as have been baptized in Christ** means that it was
by Christ's appointment that you have been instructed for
baptism: "Go ye into the whole world and preach the gos-

pel to every creature. He that believeth and is baptized shall be saved" (Mk. 16:16). In another way, **as many of you as have been baptized in Christ have put on Christ,** i.e., through a likeness and a configuration of the death of Christ: "We who are baptized in Christ Jesus are baptized in his death" (Rom. 6:3). Or: **in Christ Jesus,** i.e., in the faith of Christ. For baptism comes about only through faith, without which we derive no effect from baptism: "He that believeth and is baptized shall be saved; but he that believeth not shall be condemned" (Mk. 16:16). Or: **in Christ Jesus,** i.e., through His power and operation: "He upon whom thou shalt see the Spirit descending, he it is that baptizeth" (Jn. 1:33). Therefore, **as many of you as have been baptized** in any of those four ways **have put on Christ.**

Here it should be noted that when someone puts on clothing he is protected and covered by it and his appearance is that of the color of the clothing instead of his own. In the same way, everyone who puts on Christ is protected and covered by Christ Jesus against attack and against the heat; furthermore in such a one nothing appears except what pertains to Christ: "Put ye on the Lord Jesus Christ" (Rom. 13:14). Again, just as burning wood takes on fire and shares in fire's activity, so he who receives the virtues of Christ has put on Christ: "Stay you in the city till you be endued with power from on high" (Lk. 24:49). This applies to those who are inwardly clothed with the virtue of Christ: "Put on the new man, who according to God is created in justice and holiness of truth" (Eph. 4:24). And note that some put on Christ outwardly by good works and inwardly by a renewal of the spirit; and with respect to both they are configured to His holiness, as is mentioned in a Gloss.

He elucidates this teaching when he says, **There is neither Jew nor Greek; there is neither bond nor free: there is neither male nor female.** As if to say: Truly have I said, that **as many of you as have been baptized in Christ Jesus have put on Christ,** because there is nothing in man that would exclude anyone from the sacrament of the faith of Christ and of baptism. And he mentions three differences among men to show that no one is excluded from faith in Christ by any of them: the first difference concerns one's rite. Hence he says: **There is neither Jew nor Greek.** As if to say: Since you have been baptized in Christ, the rite from which you came to Christ, whether it was the Jewish or the Greek, is no ground for saying that anyone occupies a less honorable place in the faith: "Is he the God of the Jews only? Is he not also of the Gentiles? Yes, of the Gentiles also. For there is one God that justifieth circumcision by faith and uncircumcision through faith" (Rom. 3:29). Again: "There is no distinction of the Jew and Greek; for the same is Lord over all" (Rom. 10:12).

But this seems to militate against what is said in Romans (3:1): "What advantage then hath the Jew? Much every way." I answer that Jews and Greeks can be considered in two ways. First, according to the state in which they were before faith. In this way, the Jew was greater because of the benefits he derived from the Law. In another way, according to the state of grace; and in this way, the Jew is not greater. And this is the sense in which it is taken here.

The second difference is with respect to estate, when he says: **there is neither bond nor free,** i.e., neither slavery nor freedom, neither high estate nor low makes a difference so far as receiving the effect of baptism is concerned: "The small and great are there, and the servant is free from his master" (Job 3:19); "There is no respect of persons with God" (Rom. 2:11).

The third difference concerns the condition of the nature: **there is neither male nor female,** for sex makes no difference as far as sharing in the effect of baptism is concerned.

The underlying reason for this explanation is set forth when he says, **For you are all one in Christ Jesus.** As if to say: Truly, none of these things makes a difference in Christ, because **all of you,** i.e., believers, **are one in Christ Jesus,** because through baptism you have all been made members of Christ and you form one body, even though you are distinct individuals: "So we, being many, are one body in Christ, and everyone members one of another" (Rom. 12:5); "One body, one Spirit, as you are called in one hope of your calling" (Eph. 4:4). Now where there is unity, difference has no place. Indeed it was for this unity that Christ prayed: "That they all may be one, as thou, Father, in me, and I in thee" (Jn. 17:21).

Then when he says, **if you be Christ's, then are you the seed of Abraham, heirs according to the promise,** he argues to his main proposition in the following manner: I have said that the promises were made to Abraham and to his seed; but you are of Abraham; therefore, to you pertains the promise made to Abraham about obtaining the inheritance. Then he proves the minor premiss: You are the adopted sons of God, because by faith you are united to Christ, Who is the natural Son of God. But Christ is a son of Abraham, as was said above, **as of one, and to thy seed, which is Christ.** Therefore, if you are of Christ, i.e., in Christ, **you are the seed of Abraham,** i.e., sons, because Christ is his son. And if you are the sons, you are **heirs,** i.e., the inheritance belongs to you **according to the promise** made to Abraham: "Not they that are the children of the flesh are the children of God; but they that are the children of the promise are accounted for the seed" (Rom. 9:8).

# CHAPTER 4

1 Now, I say: As long as the heir is a child, he differeth nothing from a servant, though he be lord of all,
2 But is under tutors and governors until the time appointed by the father.
3 So we also, when we were children, were serving under the elements of the world.

After pointing out the shortcoming of the Law, the Apostle then shows here the dignity of grace. First, with a human example; secondly, with an example from Scripture (v. 21).
Regarding the first he does three things:

First, he shows the preëminence of grace over the primitive state of the Old Law by a simile taken from human law;
Secondly, he shows that they have been made partakers of this preëminence through faith (v. 6);
Thirdly, he censures them for disdaining this preëminence (v. 8).

As to the first, he does two things:

First, he lays down the simile;
Secondly, he adapts it to his proposition (v. 3).

It should be noted that the Apostle touches four things in the simile he proposes. First of all, eminence, because he speaks not of a servant but of an heir. Hence he says, **As long as the heir is a child.** This is applied and referred both to the Jewish people—who were the heirs of the promise to Abraham: "For the Lord hath chosen Jacob unto himself;

108

Israel for his own possession" (Ps. 134:4)—and to Christ, Who
is the heir of all things: "whom he hath appointed heir of all
things" (Heb. 1:2).

Secondly, smallness; hence he says, **is a child,** because
the Jews were children according to the state of the Law:
"Who shall raise up Jacob, for he is a little one?" (Am. 7:5).
Similarly, Christ, too, was become a child through the In-
carnation: "For a child is born to us and a son is given to
us" (Is. 9:6). But note that the Apostle sometimes compares
the state of the Law to a child, as he does here, and sometimes the state of the present life: "When I was a child, I
spoke as a child, I understood as a child, I thought as a
child" (1 Cor. 13:11). The reason for this is that the state
of the Old Law, because of the imperfection of knowledge,
is as a child, compared to the state of grace and truth which
came through Christ. In like manner, the state of the present
life, in which we see through a mirror in a dark manner,
is as a child, compared to the state of the future life, in
which there is perfect knowledge of God, because He is
seen as He is.

Thirdly, subjection, when he says, **he differeth nothing
from a servant, though he be lord of all: but is under tutors
and governors.** For a servant is one who is subject to a lord.
But a boy, as long as he is a child, because he does not have
fulness of knowledge and use of free will through lack of
years, is committed to the care of others who defend his
possessions—and these are called tutors—and who handle
his affairs—and these are called governors. Therefore, though
he be lord of all his things, yet, in so far as he is subject
to others, he differs nothing from a servant, because he does
not have free will but is in fact constrained. And this is
applied to the Jewish people: "And now hear, O Jacob, my
servant" (Is. 44:1).

Here it should be noted that among the Jewish people
some were servants in the strict sense; those, namely, who
observed the Law through fear of punishment and through

a desire for the temporal things which the Law promised. But there were others who were not servants in the strict sense, but living as servants, were really sons and heirs. These, although outwardly attending to temporal things and avoiding punishments, did not place their end in them but took them as a figure of spiritual goods. Hence, even though on the surface they seemed to differ nothing from servants, inasmuch as they observed the ceremonies and other commandments of the Law, they were, nevertheless, lords, because they did not use them with the same frame of mind as servants; for they used them for love of the spiritual goods they prefigured, whereas servants used them chiefly through fear of punishment and with a desire for earthly convenience. Christ, too was like a servant, because although He is the Lord of all things according to Psalm (109:1): "The Lord said to my Lord," nevertheless outwardly, as man, He seemed to differ nothing from a servant: "He emptied himself, taking the form of a servant, being made in the likeness of men, and in habit found as a man" (Phil. 2:7). Furthermore, he was under tutors and governors, because He was made under the Law, as is said below: **made under the law** (v. 4); He was also subject to men, as is said in Luke (2:51): "He was subject to them."

Fourthly, he touches on the correspondence of time, when he says, **until the time appointed by the father,** because just as the heir is under tutors for a definite period of time fixed by the father, so the Law had a time fixed by God determining how long it was to endure and how long the heir, i.e., the Jewish people, where to be under it. Similarly, there was a time fixed by the Father during which Christ was not to perform miracles or show the Lordship of His divine power: "My hour is not yet come" (Jn. 2:4).

He applies this simile when he says, **So we also, when we were children, were serving under the elements of the world.**

First, he applies it as touching the Jews;
Secondly, as touching Christ (v. 4).

He says therefore: I say that **as long as the heir is a child he differeth nothing from a servant; so, we Jews also, when we were children** in the state of the Old Law, **were serving under the elements of the world,** i.e., under the Law which promised temporal things—"If you be willing, and will hearken to me, you shall eat the good things of the land" (Is. 1:19)—and threatened temporal punishments.

Or the Old Law is called "element," because just as boys who are to be trained in a science are first taught the elements of that science and through them are brought to the fulness of science, so to the Jews was proposed the Old Law through which they would be brought to faith and justice: **the law was our pedagogue in Christ** (3:24). Or, **under the elements,** i.e., the corporeo-religious usages which they observed, such as days of the moon, new moons and the Sabbath. But one should not object that on this account they differed nothing from the pagans who served the elements of this world, for the Jews did not serve them or pay them worship; but under them they served and worshipped God, whereas the pagans in serving the elements rendered them divine worship: "They worshipped and served the creature rather than the Creator, who is blessed forever" (Rom. 1:25). Furthermore, it was necessary that the Jews serve God under the elements of this world, because such an order is in harmony with human nature which is led from sensible to intelligible things.

# CHAPTER 4

4 But, when the fulness of the time was come, God sent his Son, made of a woman, made under the law,

5 That he might redeem them who were under the law, that we might receive the adoption of sons.

Here the Apostle applies to Christ the simile he has proposed.

First, he makes the application;
Secondly, he discloses the purpose of the reality that corresponds to the simile (v. 5).

It should be noted that above, in the simile he proposed, there were four items pointed out in order, as has been said. But now, in applying them to Christ, he begins with the last, namely, the fixing of a time. The reason for this is that the time in which Christ was humiliated and in which the faithful were exalted turns out to be the same. Hence he says: **But, when the fulness of the time was come,** i.e., after the time fixed by God the Father for sending His Son had been accomplished. This is how it is taken in Luke (2:6): "Her days were accomplished, that she should be delivered." This time is called "full" because of the fulness of the graces that are given in it, according to Psalm (64:10): "The river of God is filled with water; thou hast prepared their food: for so is its preparation." Also because of the fulfillment of the figures of the Old Law: "I am not come to destroy but to fulfill" (Mt. 5:17). And because of the fulfillment of the promises: "And he shall confirm the covenant with many, in one week" (Dan. 9:27). However, the fact that he likewise

says, **But, when the fulness of time was come,** in other places
of Scripture where the time respecting Christ is said to be
accomplished, should not be explained in terms of a neces-
sity imposed by fate, but in terms of a divine ordinance,
concerning which Psalm (118:91) states: "By thy ordinance
the day goeth on; for all things serve thee."

Two reasons are given why that time was pre-ordained
for the coming of Christ. One is taken from His greatness:
for since He that was to come was great, it was fitting that
men be made ready for His coming by many indications and
many preparations. "God, who, at sundry times and in divers
manners, spoke in times past to the fathers by the prophets,
last of all in these days hath spoken to us by his Son" (Heb.
1:1). The other is taken from the role of the one coming:
for since a physician was to come, it was fitting that before
his coming, men should be keenly aware of their infirmity,
both as to their lack of knowledge during the Law of nature
and as to their lack of virtue during the written Law. Therefore it was fitting that both, namely, the Law of nature and
the written Law, precede the coming of Christ.

Secondly, he applies it as to His dignity as heir, when
he says, **God sent his Son,** namely, His own natural Son; and
if a son, then an heir also. He says, **his Son,** i.e., His own,
natural, only begotten but not adopted, Son: "God so loved
the world as to give his only begotten Son" (Jn. 3:16). **He
sent** Him, I say, without His being separated from Him, for
He was sent by assuming human nature, and yet He was in
the bosom of the Father: "The only begotten Son, Who is
in the bosom of the Father" eternally (Jn. 1:18); "And no
man hath ascended into heaven, but he that descended from
heaven, the Son of Man, who is in heaven," Who, although
He descended by assuming flesh is, nevertheless, in heaven
(Jn. 3:13). Again, He sent Him, not to be where before He
was not; because, although He came unto His own by His
presence in the flesh, yet by the presence of His Godhead,
He was in the world, as is said in John (1:14). Furthermore,

He did not send Him as a minister, because His mission was the assuming of flesh, not the putting off of majesty. God, therefore, sent His Son, I say, to heal the errantry of the concupiscible part and to illumine the ignorance of the rational part: "He sent his word and healed them: and delivered them from their destructions" (Ps. 106:20). He sent Him also to deliver them from the power of the devil against the infirmity of the irascible part: "He shall send them a Savior and defender to deliver them" (Is. 19:20). Also as a deliverer from the chains of eternal death: "I will deliver them out of the hand of death. I will redeem them from death: O death, I will be thy death" (Os. 13:14). Also to save them from their sins: "For God sent not his Son into the world to judge the world but that the world may be saved by him" (Jn. 3:17).

Thirdly, he applies the simile as to smallness, when he says, **made of a woman:** "For a child is born to us" (Is. 9:6); "He emptied himself taking the form of a servant" (Phil. 2:7). He made Himself small not by putting off greatness, but by taking on smallness.

In interpreting the passage, **made of woman,** two errors must be avoided; namely, that of Photinus, who said that Christ was solely man and received the beginning of His existence from the Virgin; in other words, that Christ was made of a woman as though deriving his beginning entirely from her. But this is false, because it contradicts what is said in Romans (1:3): "Who was made to him of the seed of David, according to the flesh"; he does not say "according to His person," which exists from eternity, namely, the hypostasis of the Son of God. Hence, just as when a shield newly comes to be white, it is not proper to say that the very substance of the shield newly came to be, but that the whiteness newly accrued to it; so from the fact that the Son of God newly assumed flesh, it is not proper to say that the **person of Christ** newly came to be, but that a human nature newly accrued to that person, as when certain things affect a body without that body itself being changed. For certain items affect a thing and change it, such as forms and absolute qualities; but certain other items affect it without changing it. Of this sort is the assuming of flesh precisely as bespeaking a relationship. Hence the person of the Word is in no way changed by it. That is why in divine matters we employ in a temporal sense terms that signify a relationship; thus, we say in Psalm (89:1): "Lord, thou hast been our refuge"; or we say that God became man. But we do not thus use forms and absolute qualities, so as to say: God was made good or wise and so on.

Secondly, one must avoid the error of Ebion, who said that Christ was born of the seed of Joseph, and who was led to this by the saying, **born of a woman.** For according to him the word "woman" always implies defloration. But this is erroneous, for in Sacred Scripture "woman" also denotes the natural sex, according to Genesis (3:12): "Adam said: The woman who thou gavest me to be my companion gave me of the tree." Here he calls her a woman while she was still a virgin.

Furthermore, by saying **made of a woman** two errors are destroyed, namely, that of Nestorious saying that Christ did not take His body of the Virgin but of the heavens and that He passed through the Blessed Virgin as through a corridor or channel. But this is false, for if it were true, He would not, as the Apostle says, have been made of a woman. By the preposition "of" [ex] the material cause is denoted. Likewise, the error of Nestorious saying that the Blessed Virgin is not the mother of the Son of God but of the son of a man. But this is shown to be false by the words of the Apostle here, that **God sent his Son made of a woman.** Now one who is made of a woman is her son. Therefore, if the Son of God was made of a woman, namely, of the Blessed Virgin, it is obvious that the Blessed Virgin is the Mother of the Son of God.

Moreover, although he might have said *"born* of a

woman," he distinctly says **made**, and not "born." Indeed, for
something to be born it must not only be produced of a
principle conjoined to it but be made from a principle separate from it. Thus a wooden chest is *made* by an artisan, but
fruit is *born* from a tree. Now the principle of human generation is twofold, namely, material—and as to this, Christ
proceeded from a conjoined principle, because He took the
matter of His body from the Virgin; and it is according to
this that He is said to be born of her: "Of whom [Mary] was
born Jesus Who is called Christ" (Mt. 1:16).—The other is
the active principle, which in the case of Christ, so far as
He had a principle, i.e., as to the forming of the body, was
not conjoined but separate, because the power of the Holy
Spirit formed it. And with respect to this He is not said to
have been born of a woman, but made, as it were, from an
extrinsic principle. From this it is obvious that the saying,
**of a woman,** does not denote a defloration; otherwise he
would have said "born" and not "made."

Fourthly, he applies the simile as to its aspect of subjection when he says, **made under the law.** But here a difficulty comes to mind from what is said below, namely: **If
you are led by the spirit, you are not under the law** (5:18).
Hence if Christ is not only spiritual but the giver of the
Spirit, it seems unbecoming to say that He was made under
the Law. I answer that "to be under the Law" can be taken
in two ways: in one way so that "under" denotes the mere
observance of the Law, and in this sense Christ was made
under the Law, because He was circumcised and presented
in the temple: "I am not come to destroy but to fulfill" (Mt.
5:17). In another way so that "under" denotes oppression.
And in this way one is said to be under the Law if he is
oppressed by fear of the Law. But neither Christ nor spiritual
men are said to be under the Law in this way.

Then when he says, **that he might redeem them who
were under the law,** he sets down the fruit of the reality in
which the simile is applied, namely, that the reason why

He willed they be subject during that time was that they might become heirs great and free. And he mentions both of these things. First, the fruit of freedom as against subjection; hence he says, **that he might redeem them who were under the law,** i.e., under the curse and burden of the Law; **Christ hath redeemed us from the curse of the law, being made a curse for us** (3:13). Secondly, the fruit of being made great, inasmuch as we are adopted as sons of God by receiving the Spirit of God and being conformed to Him: "Now if any man have not the Spirit of Christ, he is none of His" (Rom. 8:9). This adoption belongs in a special way to Christ, because we cannot become adopted sons unless we are conformed to the natural son: "For whom he foreknew, he also predestinated to be made conformable to the image of his Son" (Rom. 8:29). With this in mind, he says, **that we might receive the adoption of sons,** i.e., that through the natural Son of God we might be made adopted sons according to grace through Christ.

# CHAPTER 4

## LECTURE 3

6 And, because you are sons, God hath sent the Spirit of his Son into your hearts, crying: Abba, Father.

7 Therefore, now he is not a servant, but a son. And, if a son, an heir also through God.

Above, the Apostle revealed the gift bestowed on the Jews; here he shows that this gift pertains also to the Gentiles.

First, he mentions the gift;
Secondly, the means of obtaining it (v. 6);
Thirdly, he discloses the fruit of this gift (v. 7).

He says therefore that the gift of adoption of sons pertains not only to those who were under the Law but to the Gentiles as well. Hence he says: **because you are sons of God,** i.e., you are the sons of God, because not only the Jews but all others who believe in the Son of God are adopted as sons: "He gave them power to be made sons of God, to them that believe in his name" (Jn. 1:12). The manner in which that gift is obtained is by the sending of the Spirit of the Son of God into your hearts.

Augustine says, however, that Christ, existing in the flesh, preached in a principal manner to the Jews, but to the Gentiles as a matter of course: "For I say that Christ Jesus was minister of the circumcision for the truth of God to confirm the promises made unto the fathers" (Rom. 15:8). Accordingly, whatever pertains to the condition of the Jews is fittingly adapted to Christ.

And because they might have said that the Galatians had not been adopted as sons of God, since Christ did not assume flesh from them or preach to them, for that reason the Apostle, elucidating the manner of this adoption, says that although they were not related to Christ according to the flesh, i.e., according to race, or by reason of preaching, yet they were united to him through the Spirit and thereby adopted and made sons of God. Hence the conversion of the Gentiles is in a special way attributed to the Holy Spirit. Consequently, Peter, when he was blamed by the Jews for going to preach to the Gentiles, excused himself through the Holy Spirit, saying (Acts 11) that he could not resist the Holy Spirit by Whose inspiration he had done this. And so, because **God** the Father **sent the Spirit of his Son into** our **hearts,** i.e., the hearts of the Jews and Gentiles, we are united to Christ and by that fact are adopted as sons of God.

But it should be noted that if in certain passages of Scripture the Holy Spirit is said to be sent by the Father— "But the Paraclete, the Holy Spirit, whom the Father will send in my name" (Jn. 14:26)—and in others to be sent by the Son—"But when the Paraclete cometh, whom I will send you from the Father" (Jn. 15:26)—the Holy Spirit is none the less common to Father and Son and proceeds from Both and is sent by Both. Accordingly, wherever it is said that the Father sends the Holy Spirit, mention is made of the Son, as in the aforesaid passage: "Whom the Father will send in my name"; and where He is said to be sent by the Son, mention is made of the Father; hence He says, "Whom I will send to you from the Father." Even here, when he says, **God** the Father **hath sent the** Holy **Spirit,** mention is made at once of the Son, for he adds, **of his Son.** Nor does it matter that at times the Holy Spirit is only said to proceed from the Father, for the fact that the Son sends Him shows that He proceeds from Him. Accordingly, the Holy Spirit is called the Spirit of the Son as of the One sending and as of the One from Whom He proceeds, as well as of the One from Whom the Holy Spirit has whatever He has, just as of the Father: "He shall glorify me, because He shall receive of mine" (Jn. 16:14).

But he says, **into your hearts,** because there is a two-fold generation: one is carnal and comes about through fleshly seed sent to the place of generation. This seed, small as it is, contains in effect the whole. The other is spiritual, which comes about by spiritual seed transmitted to the place of spiritual generation, i.e., man's mind or heart, because they are born sons of God through a renewal of the mind. Furthermore, the spiritual seed is the grace of the Holy Spirit: "Whosoever is born of God sinneth not: but the generation of God preserveth him and the wicked one toucheth him not" (1 Jn. 5:18). This seed contains, in effect, the whole perfection of beatitude; hence it is called the pledge and earnest of beatitude (Eph. 1:14); "I will put a new spirit within you" (Ez. 36:26).

**Crying,** i.e., making us cry, **Abba, Father,** not with a loudness of voice but with a great fervor of love. For we cry, **Abba, Father,** when our affections are kindled by the

warmth of the Holy Spirit to desire God: "You have not received the spirit of bondage again in fear; but you have received the spirit of adoption of sons, whereby we cry, Abba
(Father)" (Rom. 8:15). **Abba** in Hebrew and **Pater** in Greek
have the same meaning of "father." And he makes mention
of both to show that the grace of the Holy Spirit, as such,
is related in a common way to both.

Then when he says, **Therefore, now he is not a servant,
but a son,** he mentions the fruit of this gift. First, as to removing all evil, from which we are freed through adoption
by the Holy Spirit. This is freedom from bondage. With respect to this he says: **Therefore,** i.e., because the Spirit cries
"Father" in us, **now,** from the time of grace, **he,** i.e., each
one of us who believes in Christ, **is not a servant,** i.e., serving in fear—"I will not now call you servants but friends"
(Jn. 15:15); "You have not received the spirit of bondage
again in fear: but you have received the spirit of adoption
of sons" (Rom. 8:15)—**but a son:** "For the Spirit himself
giveth testimony to our spirit that we are the sons of God"
(Rom. 8:16). For although we be in the condition of servants (because it is said in Luke (17:10): "When you shall
have done all these things that are commanded you, say: We
are unprofitable servants"), we are not ill-disposed servants,
i.e., serving in fear—for such a servant is deserving of torture
and chains—but we are good and faithful servants, serving
out of love. For that reason we obtain freedom through the
Son: "If, therefore, the son shall make you free, you shall
be free indeed" (Jn. 8:36).

Secondly, he mentions the fruit as to its effect of attain-
ing every good. With regard to this he says: **And, if a son,
an heir also through God:** "And if sons, heirs also: heirs
indeed of God and joint heirs with Christ" (Rom. 8:17). Now
this inheritance is the fulness of all good, for it is nothing
other than God Himself, according to Psalm (15:5): "The
Lord is the portion of my inheritance." He said to Abraham:
"I am thy reward exceeding great" (Gen. 15:1). He says,

**through God,** because as the Jews obtained the inheritance through the promise and justice of God, so the Gentiles too received it through God, i.e., through the mercy of God: "But the Gentiles are to glorify God for his mercy" (Rom. 15:9). Or, **through God,** i.e., through the working of God: "Thou hast wrought all our works for us, O Lord" (Is. 26:12).


# CHAPTER 4

### LECTURE 4


8. But then indeed, not knowing God, you served them who, by nature, are not gods.

9 But now, after that you have known God, or rather are known by God; how turn you again to the weak and needy elements which you desire to serve again?

10 You observe days and months and times, and years.

11 I am afraid of you, lest perhaps I have laboured in vain among you.

12a Be ye as I, because I also am as you.


Having disclosed the preëminence of the gift of grace and explained it with a human example, the Apostle here censures the Galatians, who scorned this grace, for being ungrateful for so great a gift.

First, he censures them for ingratitude;
Secondly, he excuses himself, explaining that he does not do this out of hatred or spite (v. 12b).

As to the first he does three things:

First, he calls to mind their earlier state;
Secondly, he extols and commends the gift they have received (v. 9);
Thirdly, he amplifies the sin committed (v. 9): **how turn you again to the weak and needy elements?**

He says therefore: **But then indeed, not knowing God, you served them who, by nature, are not gods.** As if to say: You are now sons and heirs through God; **But then indeed,** when you were heathens—"You were heretofore darkness, but now light in the Lord" (Eph. 5:8)—**not knowing God,** through lack of faith, **you served** with the worship of latria, **them who by nature are not gods,** but by the opinion of men: "You know that when you were heathens, you went to dumb idols, according as you were led" (1 Cor. 12:2); "They served the creature rather than the Creator." (Rom. 1:25). His statement, **who by nature are not gods,** serves to refute the Arians who said that Christ, the Son of God, is not God by nature. For if this were true, it would not be right to render Him latria, and whoever rendered it would be an idolater.

But someone might object that we adore the flesh and humanity of Christ; consequently, we are idolaters. I answer that even though we adore the flesh or humanity of Christ, we adore it as united to the person of the divine Word, Who is a divine hypostasis. Hence, since adoration is due to a person of the divine nature, whatever is adored in Christ is done without error.

Then when he says, **But now, after that you have known God, or rather are known by God,** he reminds them of the gift received. As if to say: If you had been ignorant and sinned, it could have been tolerated; for other things being equal, sin in a Christian is more grievous than in a pagan. But now, **since you have known God,** i.e., were brought to a knowledge of God, you sin more gravely than of old by serving and setting your hope on things you ought not: "All shall know me, from the least of them even to the greatest" (Jer. 31:34).

But the statement, **after you are known by God,** seems to cause a difficulty, for God has known all things from eternity: "All things were known to the Lord God before they were created" (Ecclus. 23:29). I answer that this is said causally, so that the sense is: **you are known by God,** i.e., God has caused you to know Him. In this way, God is said to know inasmuch as He is the cause of our knowledge. Hence, because he had previously said, **after that you have known God,** which was a true statement, he immediately amends and explains it with a figure of speech by intimating that we cannot know God of ourselves save by Him: "No man hath seen God at any time: the only begotten Son, Who is in the bosom of the Father, He hath declared him" (Jn. 1:18).

Then he upbraids them for the sin committed, saying: **how turn you again to the weak and needy elements?**

> First, he amplifies their sin;
> Secondly, he shows their imminent danger (v. 11);
> Thirdly, he draws them back to a state of safety (v. 12a).

As to the first, he does two things:

> First, he mentions the sin committed;
> Secondly, he convinces them of it (v. 10).

It should be pointed out that this passage is interpreted in two ways: in one way, that those Galatians had turned from the faith to idolatry. For this reason he says, **how turn you** from the faith **again,** i.e., a second time. "For it had been better for them not to have known the way of justice than, after they have known it, to turn back from that holy commandment which was delivered to them" (2 Pet. 2:21); "They are turned back" (Is. 42:17). **To the elements,** namely, of the world, which are **weak,** unable by themselves to subsist, because they would lapse into nothingness unless upheld by the hand which rules all things—"Upholding all things by the word of his power" (Heb. 1:3)—**and needy,** because they need God and one another to fill out the universe, **which,** namely, the elements, **you desire to serve** with the service of latria **again,** i.e., for a second time. And the proof of this is obvious, because **You observe days,** auspicious and inauspicious, **and months and times and years,** i.e., the constellations and the course of the heavenly bodies, all of which observances spring from idolatry, against which Jeremias (10:2) says: "Be not afraid of the signs of heaven which the heathens fear."

That observances of this sort are evil and contrary to the worship of the Christian religion is plain, because the distinction of days, months, years and times is based on the course of the sun and moon. Therefore, those who observe such distinctions of times are venerating heavenly bodies and arranging their activities according to the evidence of the stars, which have no direct influence on the human will or on things that depend on free will. By this practice they are put in grave danger. Hence he says: **I am afraid lest perhaps it was in vain,** i.e., fruitlessly, **that I labored among you.** Therefore the faithful must avoid observing such things. Indeed, no suggestion of these things should be found among them, for whatever is done simply out of devotion to God can turn out prosperously.

But is it never lawful to look for the influence of the stars on certain things? I answer that heavenly bodies are the cause of certain effects, namely, bodily. In such things it is lawful to consider their influence. But they are not the cause of certain other things, i.e., of things that depend on free will or on good and bad fortune. Hence in such cases to look for the influence of the stars pertains to idolatry.

But although this interpretation might be upheld, it does not accord with the Apostle's intention. For since in the entire section preceding this passage, as well as in all that follows it, he is censuring the Galatians for removing themselves from the faith and turning to the observances of the Law, it is more in keeping with his intention to expound it as referring to their turning to the legal observances. Hence he says: **After that you have known God** through faith, **how turn you** from the faith **to the elements,** i.e., to the literal observance of the Law? It is called an element, because the Law was the prime institution of divine worship. **To elements,** I say, that are **weak,** because they do not bring to perfection by

justifying: "For the law brought nothing to perfection" (Heb.
7:19), **and needy,** because they do not confer virtues and
grace or offer any help of themselves.

But what does he mean by **are you turned?** For to say
this, as well as to say, **again,** seems inappropriate, for they
neither were Jews nor had they formerly observed the Law.
I answer that the Jewish worship is midway between the
worship of the Christians and that of the Gentiles: for the
Gentiles worshipped the elements as though they were living
things; the Jews, on the other hand, did not serve the elements but served God under the elements, inasmuch as they
rendered worship to God by the observances of bodily elements: **We were serving under the elements of the world**
(v. 3); but Christians serve God under Christ, i.e., in the
faith of Christ. Now when a person reaches a terminus after
passing through the middle, if he then decides to return to
the middle, it seems to be the same as returning to the very
beginning. Therefore, because they had already reached the
terminus, namely, faith in Christ, and then returned to the
middle, i.e., to the Jewish worship, then because of a resemblance of middle to beginning, the Apostle says that they
are turned to the elements and are serving them again.

That this is so, he proves when he says: **You observe
the days** of the Jewish rite, namely, Sabbaths and the tenth
day of the month and such things, which are mentioned in
a Gloss, **and months,** i.e., new moons, as the first and seventh
month, as is had in Leviticus (Ch. 25), **and times,** namely,
of the exodus from Egypt, and the practice of going to Jerusalem three times a year, **and years** of jubilee and the seventh
year of remission. From this arises a danger because faith
in Christ profits nothing from it. Hence he says: **I am afraid
of you, lest perhaps I have labored in vain among you;** and
further on: **If you be circumcised, Christ shall profit you
nothing** (5:2).

Then when he says, **Be ye as I, because I also am as
you,** he guides them back to the state of salvation. As if to

say: I am afraid for you, lest I have labored in vain among you. But lest this be so, **Be ye as I.** In a Gloss this is taken in three ways. In the first way thus: **Be ye as I,** namely, abandon the Law as I have abandoned it. In a second way thus: **Be ye as I,** namely, correcting the old error, as I have corrected mine. And this you can do, **because I am as you,** and yet I have been corrected of my error. In the third way thus: **Be ye as I,** i.e., live without the Law, **because I,** who had the Law and was born in the Law, **am now as you** formerly were, namely, without the Law.

# CHAPTER 4

### LECTURE 5

12b Brethren, I beseech you. You have not injured me at all.
13 And you know how, through infirmity of the flesh, I preached the gospel to you heretofore; and your temptation in my flesh
14 You despised not, nor rejected; but received me as an angel of God, even as Christ Jesus.
15 Where is then your blessedness? For I bear you witness that, if it could be done, you would have plucked out your own eyes and would have given them to me.
16 Am I then become your enemy, because I tell you the truth?
17 They are zealous in your regard not well; but they would exclude you, that you might be zealous for them.
18 But be zealous for that which is good in a good thing always; and not only when I am present with you.

After censuring the Galatians, the Apostle here shows that he did not do so out of hatred. And

> First, he shows that he has no true cause of hatred toward them;
> Secondly, that he has no supposed cause (v. 16);
> Thirdly, he tells precisely why he rebuked them (v. 19).

As to the first, he does two things:

First, he shows that he has no reason for hating them;
Secondly, that contrariwise he has reason for loving them
  (v. 13).

With respect to the first it should be noted that it is
customary for a good pastor in correcting his subjects to
mingle gentleness with severity, lest they be discouraged by
too great severity. For it is written in Luke (10) that the
Samaritan in caring for the wounded man poured in oil and
wine. On the other hand, it is written of evil pastors in
Ezechiel (34:4): "You ruled over them with vigor." Therefore, as a good prelate, the Apostle shows that he does not
rebuke them in a spirit of hatred, for his words are gentle
in three respects. First, as to the charitable name he uses,
for he says, **Brethren:** "Behold how good and how pleasant
it is for brethren to dwell together in unity" (Ps. 132:1).
Secondly, as to his suppliant language, when he says: **I beseech you:** "The poor will speak with supplications" (Prov.
18:23). Thirdly, as to freeing them of blame; hence he says,
**You have not injured me at all,** and I am not the type of
person who hates those who do not offend me.

Secondly, he shows that he has reason to love them,
when he says: **you know how, through infirmity of the flesh,
I preached the gospel to you heretofore.** Here he touches
on three things that usually cause men to love one another.
The first is the mutual help of fellowship, and this is also
the cause of love being consolidated among men, according
to Luke (22:28): "And you are they who have continued
with me in my temptations; and I dispose to you as my
Father hath disposed to me, a kingdom." Touching this he
says: **And you know how, through infirmity of the flesh, I
preached the gospel to you heretofore.** Herein he does two
things:

First, he recalls the tribulation he suffered among them;
Secondly, he shows how they stood by him (v. 13).

He says, therefore, with respect to the first: I say that **You have not injured me at all;** rather you have come to my aid. **For you know,** i.e., are able to recall, **that I preached the gospel to you heretofore,** i.e., in times past, **through infirmity of the flesh,** i.e., with infirmity and affliction in my flesh, or with the many tribulations I suffered from the Jews who are of my flesh and persecuted me: "And I was with you in weakness and in fear and in much tribulation" (1 Cor. 2:3); "Power is made perfect in infirmity" (2 Cor. 12:9). And although this infirmity might have been reason for scorning me and a cause of temptation for you, according to Zacharias (13:7): "Strike the shepherd and the sheep will be scattered": nevertheless, **your temptation,** which was **in my flesh,** i.e., my tribulation, which was a source of temptation for you, **you despised not:** "Despise not a man for his look" (Ecclus. 11:2) because as the Lord says in Luke (10:16): "He that despiseth you, despiseth me." **Neither did you reject me** and my teaching, but you were willing to share my tribulations: "Woe to you that despisest, shall you not also be despised?" (Is. 33:1).

The second thing that strengthens love among men is mutual love and affection toward one another, according to Proverbs (8:17): "I love them that love me." As to this he says: **but you received me as an angel of God,** i.e., with the honor accorded to a messenger announcing God's words: "When you received of us the word of the hearing of God, you received it not as the word of men but (as it is indeed) the word of God" (1 Thess. 2:13). For this reason preachers are called angels: "They shall seek the law at the priest's mouth, because he is the angel of the Lord of hosts" (Mal. 2:7). And not only as an angel did you receive me, but **even as Christ Jesus,** i.e., as though Christ Himself had come, Who, indeed, had come to them in him and spoke in him, according to 2 Corinthians (13:3): "Do you seek a proof of Christ that speaketh in me?" "He that receiveth you receiveth me" (Mt. 10:40). But he then rebukes them for their change

of heart; hence he says, **Where is then your blessedness?** As
if to say: Did not men think you blessed for honoring me
and accepting my preaching? "Where is thy fear, thy forti-
tude, thy patience and the perfection of thy ways?" (Job
4:6).

The third thing that strengthens love is doing good to
one another. As to this he says: **For I bear you witness that,
if it could be done,** i.e., had been just to do so (for that can
be done which it is just to do) or had been to the advantage of the Church, **you would have plucked out your own
eyes and would have given them to me.** As if to say: You
loved me so much that you would have given me not only
your external goods but your very eyes.

Then when he says: **Am I then become your enemy,
because I tell you the truth?**, he states the cause of a supposed hatred.

First, the cause on the part of the Apostle;
Secondly, on the part of the false brethren (v. 17).

He says therefore: If you have done me so much good,
are you to believe that **I am become your enemy because
I tell you the truth?** The word **enemy** used here can be interpreted in two ways: in one way as meaning that he hates
them; in this case the interpretation is **have I become your
enemy,** i.e., hate you? Hence what follows, namely, **because
I tell you the truth,** can be taken as an indication of hatred,
even though telling the truth at the proper time and place
is a sign of love. In another way, the word **enemy** can be
taken in a passive sense, i.e., so that he is hated by them;
then **have I become your enemy** is interpreted as **Do you
hate me?** and this because I tell you the truth, so that telling the truth is set down as the cause of hatred. For men
who tell the truth are hated by evil men, since the truth
engenders hatred: "They have hated him that rebuketh in
the gate: and I have abhorred him that speaketh perfectly"
(Am. 5:10).

But on the other hand, it is said in Proverbs (28:23): "He that rebuketh a man shall afterward find favor with him more then he that by a flattering tongue deceiveth him." I answer that the solution to this can be gathered from what is said in Proverbs (9:9): "Rebuke not a scorner, lest he hate thee. Rebuke a wise man and he will love thee." For if the one corrected loves the corrector, it is a sign of virtue; conversely, it is a sign of malice, if he should hate him. For since a man naturally hates what is contrary to what he loves, then if you hate one who corrects you for evil, it is obvious that you love the evil; but if you love him, you indicate that you hate sin. For at first, when men are corrected, they are attached to their sins—that is why a sinner's first reaction is to hate the one correcting him; but after the correction he puts aside his attachment to sin and loves the one correcting him. And therefore the passage from Proverbs expressly says that later he will find favor with him.

Then when he says, **They are zealous in your regard not well,** he states another supposed cause, namely, on the part of the false brethren.

First, he states it;
Secondly, he refutes it (v. 18).

As to the first it should be noted that, as has been said above, certain false brethren, converted from Judaism, went about the churches of the Gentiles, preaching the observance of the Law. Because Paul opposed them, they slandered him. They did this not so much with an eye to their salvation as to get rid of Paul. Hence the Apostle says, **They are zealous in your regard,** i.e., they do not allow you (whom they love with a love not of friendship but of self-interest) to associate with us. For jealous rivalry is zeal that arises from any love whatsoever and does not brook what is loved to be shared. But because their love for them was not good: first of all, because they did not love them so as to advantage them but for their own gain—and this is obvious from the fact that they wanted to keep the Apostle away from them as one opposed to their own advantage—and secondly, because this was a source of harm to the Gentiles—for they sought from them an advantage by which the latter would suffer harm; for these reasons he says, **They are zealous in your regard** but **not well,** because they are not interested in your welfare. And this is obvious, because **they would exclude you that you might be zealous for them,** i.e., that you might admit none but them: "Envy not the unjust man and do not follow his ways" (Prov. 3:31); "Let not thy heart envy sinners" (Prov. 23:17).

But he rejects this when he says, **But be zealous for that which is good in a good thing always.** As if to say: You ought not to be zealous for them in their teaching; but be zealous for a good teacher, i.e., for me and those like me: "And who is he that can hurt you if you be zealous of the good?" (1 Pet. 3:13). But because there can be evil in a good teacher, he adds, **be zealous of the good** teacher, yet I say **in a good thing,** i.e., in that which is good: "Follow after charity and be zealous for spiritual goods" (1 Cor. 14:1).

Now, although the Apostle speaks of himself, according to a Gloss, when he says, **be zealous of the good,** yet he adds **in a good thing,** because as he says: "I am not conscious of any thing, yet I am not hereby justified" (1 Cor. 4:4). But because some are zealous for a good teacher in his presence alone, he adds: **always, and not only when I am present with you;** because zeal for the good, if it continues even when the teacher is absent, is an indication that it proceeds from love and fear of God Who sees all: "Servants, obey in all things your masters according to the flesh, not serving to the eye, as pleasing men, but in simplicity of heart, fearing God" (Col. 3:22).

# CHAPTER 4

### LECTURE 6

19 My little children, of whom I am in labour again, until Christ be formed in you.

20 And I would willingly be present with you now and change my voice; because I am ashamed for you.

Above, the Apostle dismissed the false cause of his correcting the Galatians; here he discloses the true cause, which is sorrow for their imperfection.

First, he expresses the heartfelt sorrow of which he spoke;
Secondly, a desire to manifest this sorrow (v. 20);
Thirdly, he gives the cause of the sorrow (v. 20): **because I am ashamed for you.**

This sorrow proceeded from charity, because he grieved for their sins: "I beheld the transgressors and I pined away; because they kept not thy word" (Ps. 118:158). And so he addresses them in words of charity, saying, **My little children.** He purposely does not call them sons, but little children, to indicate the imperfection whereby they had become small: "As unto little ones in Christ, I gave you milk to drink, not meat" (1 Cor. 3:1).

It should be noted that during parturition a child is called a little one. And this is what they were, because they needed to be born again, even though parents according to the flesh bring forth their child only once. Accordingly he says to them, **of whom I am in labor again.** For he was in labor of them during their first conversion; but since they had now turned from the one who called them, to another gospel, they needed to be brought forth anew. Hence he says, **I am in**

**labor,** i.e., with labor and pain I bring them forth into the light of faith. In these words the Apostle bares his grief. Hence a man's conversion is called a birth: "They bow themselves to bring forth young" (Job 39:3); "And being with child she cried, travailing in birth and was in pain to be delivered" (Apoc. 12:2). Therefore it is because of his pain that he rebukes them so sharply, as a woman cries aloud because of the pains of childbirth: "I will speak now as a woman in labor" (Is. 42:14).

The reason for the iterated travail is that you are not perfectly formed. Hence he says: **until Christ be formed in you,** i.e., until you receive His likeness, which you have lost through your sin. He does not say, "That you may be formed in Christ," but **until Christ be formed in you,** to make it resound more terrifyingly on their ears. For Christ is formed in the heart by "formed faith": "That Christ might dwell in your hearts by faith" (Eph. 3:17). But when one does not have "formed faith," Christ has already died in him: "Until the day dawn and the day star arise in your hearts" (2 Petr. 1:19). Thus Christ grows in a man according to his progress in the faith; conversely, as it diminishes, He recedes. Therefore, when the faith of a man is rendered "unformed" by sin, Christ is not formed in him; and so, because there was not a formed faith in them, they needed to be brought forth in the womb again until Christ be formed in them through faith, i.e., "formed faith," which works through love. Or, **until Christ be formed in you,** i.e., through you Christ appear finely formed to others.

Here someone might say: "Away from us you say these things, but if you were with us, you would not say them," according to 2 Corinthians (10:10): "His bodily presence is weak and his speech contemptible." Therefore, he expresses a desire to manifest his grief more vividly, saying, **I would willingly be present with you now and change my voice.** As if to say: I use gentle language now, calling you friends and sons, in my absence; but if I were present among you, I would correct you more sharply. For if I were present and speaking the things I am now writing in a letter, the correction would be more severe; because I would then be able to express the scolding tones of my rebuke and the cries of my anger and the pain in my heart, much better than I can convey them by letter. And a living voice would more effectively stir your hearts to shame for your error and my anxiety.

And the cause of this sorrow is that **I am ashamed for you,** i.e., I blush for you in the presence of others; for as it is said in Ecclesiasticus (22:3): "A son ill taught is the confusion of the father." For since a son is a thing of the father, and a disciple as such is a thing of his master, a master rejoices in the good he sees reflected in him and glories in it as though it were his own. Conversely, he is pained at evil and is ashamed. Hence because they had been turned from good to evil, for that reason the Apostle is ashamed.

# CHAPTER 4

## LECTURE 7

21 Tell me, you that desire to be under the law, have you not read the law?
22 For it is written that Abraham had two sons: the one by a bondwoman and the other by a free woman.
23 But he who was of the bondwoman was born according to the flesh; but he of the free woman was by promise.
24a Which things are said by an allegory.

Above, the Apostle showed the preëminence of grace by a human example; here he proves it on the authority of the Scripture.

First, he proposes a fact;
Secondly, he expounds its mystery (v. 24);
Thirdly, he concludes his proposition (v. 31).

As to the first, he does two things:

First, he elicits their attention;
Secondly, he sets forth his intention (v. 22).

He says therefore: **Tell me, you that desire to be under the law, have you not read the law?** As if to say: If you are wise, consider my objections; if you cannot answer them, yield: "Answer, I beseech you, without contention: and speaking that which is just, answer me" (Job 6:29). Now I raise this objection to you. You have either read the Law or not. If you have read it, you ought to know the things written in it. But those things prove that it should be abandoned. If you have not read it, you ought not accept what you do not know: "Let thy eyelids go before thy steps" (Prov. 4:25). He says **under the law,** i.e., under the burden of the Law. For to shoulder something light is not a feat; but to assume a heavy burden, such as the burden of the Law, seems to be a mark of exceeding stupidity: "This is a yoke which neither our fathers nor we have been able to bear" (Ac. 15:10); which is to be understood of those who wish to live according to the flesh under the Law.

Then when he says, **It is written that Abraham had two sons,** he sets forth his intention, saying: The reason I ask whether you have read the Law is that it contains certain things which clearly indicate that the Law must not be retained. And the Apostle mentions specifically the two sons of Abraham. First, he states one point in which they are alike. Secondly, two points in which they differ.

They are alike in having the same father. Hence he says, **It is written that Abraham had two sons.** In fact he had more than two, because after Sara's death, he fathered other sons of Cetura, as is stated in Genesis (Ch. 25). But the Apostle does not mention them because they have no role in this allegory. Now two peoples, the Jews and the Gentiles, can be signified by those two, i.e., the son of the bondwoman and the son of the free woman—and by the other sons of Cetura,

schismatics and heretics. These two peoples are alike in having one father, for the Jews are the children of Abraham according to the flesh, but the Gentiles, by imitating him in
faith. Or, they are the sons of Abraham, i.e., of God, Who
is the Father of all: "Have we not all one father?" (Mal.
2:10); "Is he the God of the Jews only?" (Rom. 3:29).

But they differ in two respects: namely, in the condition
of their mother, because one is of a bondwoman, as is said
in Genesis (Ch. 21) (yet Abraham did not sin by lying with
her, because he approached her in conjugal affection and
under God's ordinance); the other, namely, Isaac, whom Sara,
his wife, begot unto him was born of a free woman: "I will
return and come to thee at this time, life accompanying, and
Sara thy wife shall have a son" (Gen. 18:10). Also, they
differ as to the manner of procreation, because the son of
the bondwoman, i.e., Ismael, was born according to the flesh,
but the one of the free woman, i.e., Isaac, according to the
promise.

Here a twofold misinterpretation must be avoided. The
first is lest we understand **born according to the flesh** as
though "flesh" refers here to an act of sin, as it does in Romans (8:13): "If you live according to the flesh, you shall
die," and 2 Corinthians (10:3): "For although we walk in
the flesh, we do not war according to the flesh"—as though
Abraham sinned in begetting Ismael. The other is lest we
suppose, when it is said, **by promise,** that Isaac was not born
according to the flesh, i.e., through a carnal union, but by
the Holy Spirit.

Therefore, it must be said that Ismael was born according to the flesh, i.e., according to the nature of the flesh. For
it is natural among men that from a fertile young woman,
such as Agar was, and a man advanced in years a son be
born. But that Isaac be born according to promise is beyond
the nature of the flesh: for the nature of the flesh cannot
achieve that a son be born of an old man and a barren old
woman, as Sara was. In Ismael are signified the Jewish peo-

ple, who were born according to the flesh; in Isaac are signified the Gentiles, who were born according to the promise, in which Abraham was promised that he would be the father of many nations: "In thy seed shall all the nations of the earth be blessed" (Gen. 22:18).

Then he discloses the mystery when he says, **Which things are said by an allegory.**

First, he tells what sort of mystery it is;
Secondly, he explains it (v. 24).

He says therefore: These things which are written about the two sons **are said by an allegory,** i.e., the understanding of one thing under the image of another. For an allegory is a figure of speech or a manner of narrating, in which one thing is said and something else is understood. Hence "allegory" is derived from "alos" (alien) and "goge" (a leading), leading, as it were, to a different understanding.

Here it should be noted that "allegory" is sometimes taken for any mystical meaning: sometimes for only one of the four, which are the historical, allegorical, mystical and the anagogical, which are the four senses of Sacred Scripture, all of which differ in signification. For signification is twofold: one is through words; the other through the things signified by the words. And this is peculiar to the sacred writings and no others, since their author is God in Whose power it lies not only to employ words to signify (which man can also do), but things as well. Consequently, in the other sciences handed down by men, in which only words can be employed to signify, the words alone signify. But it is peculiar to Scripture that words and the very things signified by them signify something. Consequently this science can have many senses. For that signification by which the *words* signify something pertains to the *literal* or *historical* sense. But the signification whereby the things signified by the words further signify other things pertains to the *mystical* sense.

There are two ways in which something can be signified by the literal sense: either according to the usual construction, as when I say, "the man smiles"; or according to a likeness or metaphor, as when I say, "the meadow smiles." Both of these are used in Sacred Scripture; as when we say, according to the first, that Jesus ascended, and when we say according to the second, that He sits at the right hand of God. Therefore, under the literal sense is included the parabolic or metaphorical.

However, the mystical or spiritual sense is divided into three types. First, as when the Apostle says that the Old Law is the figure of the New Law. Hence, insofar as the things of the Old Law signify things of the New Law, it is the *allegorical* sense. Then, according to Dionysius in the book *On The Heavenly Hierarchy,* the New Law is a figure of future glory; accordingly, insofar as things in the New Law and in Christ signify things which are in heaven, it is the *anagogical* sense. Furthermore, in the New Law the things performed by the Head are examples of things we ought to do—because "What things soever were written were written for our learning" (Rom. 15:3)—accordingly insofar as the things which in the New Law were done in Christ and done in things that signify Christ are signs of things we ought to do, it is the *moral* sense. Examples will clarify each of these. For when I say, "Let there be light," referring literally to corporeal light, it is the literal sense. But if it be taken to mean "Let Christ be born in the Church," it pertains to the allegorical sense. But if one says, "Let there be light," i.e., "Let us be conducted to glory through Christ," it pertains to the anagogical sense. Finally, if it is said "Let there be light," i.e., "Let us be illumined in mind and inflamed in heart through Christ," it pertains to the moral sense.

# CHAPTER 4

## LECTURE 8

24b For these are the two testaments. The one from mount Sinai, engendering unto bondage, which is Agar.

25 For Sinai is a mountain in Arabia, which hath affinity to that Jerusalem which now is, and is in bondage with her children.

26 But that Jerusalem which is above is free; which is our mother.

27 For it is written: Rejoice thou barren, that bearest not; break forth and cry, thou that travailest not; for many are the children of the desolate, more than of her that hath a husband.

Above, the Apostle spoke of the mystical sense; here he discloses the mystery:

First, as to the mothers;
Secondly, as to the sons (v. 28).

By the two mothers he understands the two testaments. Therefore,

First, he states the thing signified;
Secondly, he explains it (v. 24): **The one from mount Sinai.**

He says therefore, **These,** i.e., the two wives, the bond-woman and the free woman, **are the two testaments,** the Old and the New: "I will make with the house of Israel a new covenant" (behold, the New Testament), "not according to the covenant which I made with their fathers" (behold the Old Testament) (Jer. 31:31). For the free woman signifies the New Testament and the bondwoman the Old.

To understand what a testament is, we should consider that a testament is a pact or agreement dealing with matters which are confirmed by witnesses. Hence in Scripture in many places in lieu of testament is put pact or agreement. Now, whenever a pact or agreement is struck, a promise is made. Therefore, according to the diversity of promises there is a diversity of testaments. But two things have been promised to us: temporal things in the Old Law, and eternal things in the New: "Rejoice and be glad because your reward is great in heaven" (Mt. 5:12). Hence these two promises are the two testaments. Hence the Apostle, when he says, **The one from mount Sinai, engendering unto bondage**, explains them.

First, as to the Old;
Secondly, as to the New (v. 26).

To understand this text, it must be noted with respect to the first that a citizen of a city is called its son, and the city itself his mother: "Daughters of Jerusalem, weep not for me" (Lk. 23:28); "The noble sons of Sion" (Lam. 4:2). Therefore, by the fact that certain ones become citizens of a city, they are made its sons. Now there is a twofold city of God: the one of earth, called the earthly Jerusalem, and the other of Heaven, called the heavenly Jerusalem. Furthermore, men were made citizens of the earthly city through the Old Testament, but of the heavenly through the New. Therefore as to this he does two things:

First, he expounds the mystery;
Secondly, he accounts for the mystical explanation (v. 25).

He says therefore first: I say that it signifies the two Testaments, namely, the Old and the New. And with respect to this he says: **The one from mount Sinai, engendering unto bondage.** Wherein is mentioned first of all the place in which it was given, namely, on Mount Sinai, as is recorded in Exodus (Ch. 20). According to a Gloss the mystical rendition of this is that Sinai is interpreted "commandment." Hence in Ephe-

sians (Ch. 2) the Old Law is called by the Apostle the law
of the Commandments. Now a mountain signifies pride: "Before your feet stumble upon the dark mountains" (Jer. 13:16).
Hence by this mountain on which the Law was given a twofold pride of the Jews is signified: one by which they were
arrogant against God: "I know thy obstinacy and thy most
stiff neck" (Deut. 31:27); the other by which they boasted
at the expense of other nations, thus perverting what is said
in Psalm (147:20): "He hath not done in like manner to
every nation; and his judgments he hath not made manifest
to them."

Secondly, he explains the end for which it was given,
namely, not to make them free, but to make them children
of a bondwoman, **engendering unto bondage, which is Agar,**
i.e., which is signified by Agar, who engenders unto bondage,
namely, the Old Testament. And this it does with respect to
three things; namely, feeling, understanding and fruit. As to
understanding, indeed, according to knowledge: because in
man is a twofold knowledge. One is free, when he knows the
truth of things according to themselves; the other is servile,
i.e., veiled under figures, as was the knowledge of the Old
Testament. As to feeling, the New Law engenders the feeling
of love, which pertains to freedom: for one who loves is moved
by his own initiative. The Old, on the other hand, engenders
the feeling of fear in which is servitude; for one who fears
is moved not by his own initiative but by that of another:
"You have not received the spirit of bondage again in fear;
but you have received the spirit of adoption of sons" (Rom.
8:15). But as to the fruit, the New Law begets sons to whom
is owed the inheritance, whereas to those whom the Old Law
engenders are owed small presents as to servants: "The servant abideth not in the house forever; but the son abideth
forever" (Jn. 8:35).

Then he gives the explanation of the mystery when he
says: **Sinai is a mountain in Arabia, which hath affinity to
that Jerusalem which now is, and is in bondage with her**

**children.** But here a difficulty arises: for since Sinai is almost twenty days journey from Jerusalem, it seems false that Sinai has affinity to [borders on] Jerusalem, as the Apostle says here. To this a Gloss responds in a mystical manner that Sinai is in Arabia, which stands for the abjection or affliction under which the Old Testament was given, because the men under it were oppressed by carnal observances after the manner of slaves and foreigners: "This is a yoke which neither we nor our fathers were able to bear" (Ac. 15:10). This mountain neighbors on Jerusalem not by a spatial continuity but by a likeness **to that Jerusalem which now is,** i.e., to the Jewish people, because just as they love earthly things and for the sake of temporal things are under the bondage of sin, so that mountain engendered unto bondage.

But this does not seem to be the Apostle's intention. For he wants to bring out that from the very place of bondage the Old Testament, which was given on Mount Sinai, engenders unto bondage, because it was given on Sinai not as a place where the children of Israel were to remain, but as a stage in their journey to the promised land. For Jerusalem, too, engenders sons unto bondage. Hence it is with respect to this that Mount Sinai is continuous with her. And this is what he says: **which hath affinity to that** (i.e., by being part of the continuous route followed by those going to Jerusalem) **Jerusalem which now is, and is in bondage with her children,** i.e., the bondage of legal observances (from which Christ redeemed us) and of various sins—"He that commits sins is the servant of sin" (Jn. 8:34)—and, literally, from bondage under the Romans who were their masters.

Then when he says, **But that Jerusalem which is above is free,** he discloses the mystery of the free woman.

First, he discloses the mystery;
Secondly, he refers to a prophecy (v. 27).

The first can be understood in two ways, accordingly as we understand this mother to be the one by whom we are engendered, which is the Church Militant, or the mother whose sons we become, which is the Church Triumphant: "He hath regenerated us unto a lively hope by the resurrection of Jesus Christ from the dead" (1 Pet. 1:3). Hence we are so generated in the present Church Militant as to arrive at the Triumphant. Therefore in explaining it thus, our mother is described by four things: by her sublimity, when he says, **above;** secondly, by name, when he says, **Jerusalem;** thirdly by her freedom, when he says, **is free;** fourthly, by her fecundity when he says, **our mother.**

She is sublime on account of the face to face vision of God and the perfect enjoyment of God; and this, as to the Church Triumphant: "Then shalt thou see, and abound, and thy heart shall wonder and be enlarged" (Is. 60:5); "Mind the things that are above" (Col. 3:2). Again she is sublime through faith and hope as to the Church Militant: "Our conversation is in heaven" (Phil. 3:20); "Who is this that cometh up from the desert, flowing with delights?" (Cant. 8:5). Further, she is a peacemaker, because she is **Jerusalem,** i.e., vision of peace. This belongs to the Church Triumphant as having perfect peace: "Who hath placed peace in thy borders" (Ps. 147:14); "My people shall sit in the beauty of peace" (Is. 32:18). Likewise it pertains to the Church Militant which possesses the peace of resting in Christ: "In me you shall have peace" (Jn. 16:33). Furthermore, she is free: "Because the creature also itself shall be delivered from the servitude of corruption" (Rom. 8:21). And this both as to the Church Triumphant and the Church Militant according to Apoc. (21:2): "I saw the holy city, the new Jerusalem, coming down out of heaven from God." Finally, she is fruitful, because she is our mother: Militant as engendering; Triumphant as the one whose sons we become: "Shall Sion say: This man and that man is born of her" (Ps. 86:5); "Thy sons shall come from afar, and thy daughters shall rise up at thy side" (Is. 60:4).

**For it is written,** namely in Isaias (54:1) according to the Septuagint. Here is mentioned the prophecy through which is proved, first of all, that the mother referred to is free, and secondly, that she is fruitful. With respect to the first, it should be noted that in a fertile woman there is first sorrow in giving birth, but this is followed by joy in beholding the child: "A woman when she is in labor hath sorrow, because her hour is come; but when she hath brought forth the child, she remembereth no more her anguish for joy that a man is born into the world" (Jn. 16:21). But a barren woman neither suffers the pangs of birth nor has joy in a child. Again there is a difference between bearing and travailing. For the latter refers to the effort to bear, whereas the former refers to the releasing of the foetus now formed. Therefore the fertile woman experiences pain in travail but joy in bearing; the sterile woman, on the other hand, experiences neither the pain of travail nor the joy of bearing.

But these are the two things which the prophet announces to the barren woman: **Rejoice, thou barren, that bearest not: break forth and cry, thou that travailest not.** Herein he speaks of Jerusalem, which he calls free and is signified by the barren Sara. For the Church was barren, namely, the Church Militant, of the Gentiles before their conversion when they offered their sons not to God but to the devil. Hence it is said to Babylon: "Barrenness and widowhood will come upon thee, because of the multitude of thy sorceries" (Is. 47:9). The Church Triumphant, too, was barren before the passion of Christ, because to her were born no sons who entered into glory, save in hope. For a mighty engine of war blocked the entrance to Paradise, so that no one might enter. To this barren one he says: **Rejoice thou that bearest not.** As if to say: The barren, as has been said, are sorrowful, not because they bear, but because they bear not: "As Anna had her heart full of grief, she prayed to the Lord, shedding many tears" (1 Kg. 1:10). But you shall rejoice in the great number of your children: "Then shall thy heart wonder and be enlarged," i.e., you will show the joy in your soul outwardly (Is. 60:5). For there are two things in childbirth: the pain from the rupturing of the membrane enclosing the child in the womb, and the crying from pain. Hence he says, **thou that travailest not,** i.e., the Church Militant, that makes no effort to bear through desire, and the Church Triumphant, that does not cry for travail; or because the time for having sons has not yet come, **break forth,** i.e., show outwardly the joy you have within and cry with sounds of praise: "Cry, cease not, lift up thy voice like a trumpet" (Is. 58:1). These two things, namely, to cry and to break forth, pertain to freedom.—Thus the freedom of the mother is made manifest.

He follows with the fruitfulness: **for many are the children of the desolate, more than of her that hath a husband.** But since it was said above that the free Church is signified by Sara, there seems to be some doubt whether Sara was desolate. I answer that she was made desolate by Abraham, as it is said here, not by a divorce but with respect to the work of the flesh. For Abraham resorted to the work of the flesh not for the pleasure but to obtain a child. Therefore when he learned that Sara was barren, he abandoned her; not by forsaking the marriage bed, but by not resorting to her from precisely the time that Sara introduced the bondwoman to him. By this we are given to understand that the Church of the Gentiles was left desolate by Christ, because Christ had not yet come; and that the Church Triumphant was desolate of men, for whom no means of entry was open. Of this desolate woman, i.e., the Church of the Gentiles, there are many children, i.e., **more than of her,** namely, the synagogue, **that hath a husband,** namely, Moses: "The barren hath borne many: and she that had many children is weakened" (1 Kg. 2:5). And this is due to the coming of the spouse, namely, Christ, by Whom she had been left desolate, not by want of love, but because the bearing of children had been delayed.

# CHAPTER 4

## LECTURE 9

28 Now we, brethren, as Isaac was, are the children of promise.
29 But as then he that was born according to the flesh persecuted
him that was after the spirit; so also it is now.
30 But what saith the scripture? Cast out the bondwoman and her
son; for the son of the bondwoman shall not be heir with the son of
the free woman.
31 So then, brethren, we are not the children of the bondwoman
but of the free; by the freedom wherewith Christ has made us free.

Having disclosed the mystery as to the mothers, he now
discloses it as to the sons.

First, he differentiates between the sons;
Secondly, he sets down the main conclusion (v. 31).

He distinguishes the sons on three counts:

First, as to the manner of origin;
Secondly, as to the feeling of love (v. 29);
Thirdly, as to their right to the inheritance (v. 30).

The manner of origin, according to which the sons of
Abraham are born, is twofold: one is by origin according to
the flesh, as Ismael, of the bondwoman; the other not according to the flesh, as Isaac, of the free woman—not because he was not born in the way of nature, but because,
as has been said, it was beyond the natural power of the
flesh for a son to be born of a barren old woman. Two people are understood by these two sons: by Işmael is understood the Jewish people, who derived from Abraham by carnal
propagation; but by Isaac, the people of the Gentiles, who
descended from Abraham by imitation of his faith. Hence he

says: **Now we, brethren,** i.e., the faithful, both Jew and Gentile, **as Isaac was,** i.e., in the line of Isaac, **are the children of the promise** that was made to Abraham: "They that are the children of the promise are accounted for the seed" (Gen. 21; Rom. 9:8). But note that the children of Abraham according to the flesh are, literally, the Jewish people; but, mystically, the ones who come to the faith for the sake of carnal and temporal goods.

Secondly, they are distinguished according to affection, because **he that was born according to the flesh persecuted him that was after the spirit.** But this raises a difficulty. First, because it is not recorded that Ismael persecuted Isaac, but only that they played together: "When Sara had seen the son of Agar, the Egyptian, playing with Isaac her son, she said to Abraham: Cast out this bondwoman and her son" (Gen. 21:9). I answer that the Apostle calls this playing a persecution, because there is deception when an older person plays with a younger one; since the older person, in playing with the younger, intends to deceive him. Or, as some say, Ismael compelled Isaac to adore the clay images he fashioned. By this he was teaching him to be turned from the worship of the one God; and this was a considerable persecution, since it is a greater evil to cause spiritual death than bodily. Furthermore, in Genesis this is called a game because he did this under the guise of a game.

There is another difficulty, namely, how the children according to the flesh persecuted and do persecute the children according to the spirit? The answer is that from the beginning of the early Church the Jews persecuted Christians, as is obvious in the Acts of the Apostles, and they would do the same even now, if they were able. Now, however, those who are carnal persecute spiritual men in the Church even as to the body; those, namely, who seek glory and temporal gain in the Church. Hence a Gloss says that "all who seek from the Lord earthly aggrandizement in the Church pertain to this Ismael. They are the ones who oppose those who are making spiritual progress and slander them. They have iniquity in their mouth, and craft and deceit on their tongues." But the ones who spiritually persecute the spiritual sons are the haughty and the hypocrites. For sometimes they who are plainly carnal and evil recognize their guilt and humble themselves before the good; but the foolish persecute in others the goodness they themselves lack.

A further question arises from the fact that heretics whom we persecute say that they are the ones born according to the spirit and we according to the flesh. I answer that there are two kinds of persecution: the good one is that in which a person persecutes another to lead him back to good. And this is what just men do to evil men, and spiritual men to carnal men; either to correct them, if they want to be converted, or, if they are obstinate, to destroy them, lest they contaminate the flock of the Lord. The other type of persecution is evil, namely, when a person persecutes another in order to pervert him; and this is what those who are born according to the flesh do to those who are born according to the spirit.

Finally, as to their right to the inheritance, they are distinguished by the authority of Scripture: **Cast out the bond-woman and her son** (Gen. 21:10). By this we are given to understand that the Jews and persecutors of the Christian religion, as well as carnal and evil Christians, will be cast out from the kingdom of heaven: "Many shall come from the east and the west and shall sit down with Abraham and Isaac and Jacob in the kingdom of heaven" (Mt. 8:11); "Without are dogs and sorcerers" (Apoc. 22:15). Furthermore, the bondwoman, i.e., vice and sin itself, will be cast out: "Every work that is corruptible shall fail in the end" (Ecclus. 14:20). The reason for all this is added, **because the son of the bondwoman shall not be heir with the son of the free woman.** For in this world the good are mingled with the wicked and the wicked with the good: "As the lily among thorns, so is my love among the daughters" (Cant. 2:2). But

in the eternal fatherland there will be only the good. In
Judges (11:2) it is said to Jephte: "Thou canst not inherit
in the house of our father, because thou art born of a harlot."
This freedom we obtain from Christ; hence he says, **by the
freedom wherewith Christ has made us free:** "If therefore
the son shall make you free, you shall be free indeed" (Jn.
8:36).

# CHAPTER 5

1 Stand fast and be not held again under the yoke of bondage.

2 Behold, I, Paul, tell you, that if you be circumcised, Christ shall profit you nothing.

3 And I testify again to every man circumcising himself that he is a debtor to do the whole law.

4 You are made void of Christ, you who are justified in the law; you are fallen from grace.

Above, the Apostle showed that justice is not through the Law; here he leads them back from error to a state of rectitude.

First, with respect to divine matters.
Secondly, with respect to human affairs (6:1).

As to the first, he does two things:

First, he admonishes them;
Secondly, he gives the reason underlying his admonition (v. 2).

In the admonition itself he includes two things: one is an inducement to good: the other is a caution against evil. He induces to good when he says, **Stand fast.** As if to say: Since you have been set free from the bondage of the Law through Christ, stand fast and, with your faith firm and feet planted, persevere in freedom. And so when he says, **Stand fast,** he exhorts them to rectitude. For he that stands is erect: "He that thinketh himself to stand, let him take heed, lest he fall" (1 Cor. 10:12). Likewise he exhorts them to be firm: "Therefore, be ye steadfast and unmoveable" (1 Cor. 15:58);

150

"Stand, therefore, having your loins girt about with truth"
(Eph. 6:14).

But he cautions and draws them from evil, when he adds:
**and be not held again under the yoke of bondage,** i.e., do
not subject yourself to the Law which engenders unto bondage. Of this yoke, it is written in Acts (15:10): "This is a
yoke which neither we nor our fathers have been able to
bear," a yoke from which we have been loosed by Christ
alone: "For the yoke of their burden, and the rod of their
shoulder, and the sceptre of their oppressor, thou hast overcome" (Is. 9:4). The reason for adding, **again,** is not that
they had been under the Law before, but that, as Jerome
says, to observe the legal ceremonies after the Gospel is so
great a sin as to border on idolatry. Hence, because they
had been idolaters, if they were to submit themselves to the
yoke of circumcision and the other legal observances, they
would be, as it were, returning to the very things wherein
they had formerly practiced idolatry.

However, according to Augustine in *Epistle 19,* three
periods of time are distinguished with respect to the observance of the legal ceremonies: namely, the time before the
passion, the time before the spreading of grace and the time
after the spreading of grace. To observe the legal ceremonies
after grace had been preached is a mortal sin for the Jews.
But during the interim, i.e., before the preaching of grace,
they could be observed without sin even by those who had
been converted from Judaism, provided they set no hope on
them. However, those converted from paganism could not
observe them without sin. Therefore, because the Galatians
had not come from Judaism but wanted, nevertheless, to observe the legal ceremonies and put their hope in them, they
were in effect returning to the yoke of bondage. For in their
case, observances of this sort were akin to idolatry, inasmuch
as they entertained a false notion touching Christ, believing
that salvation cannot be obtained by Him without the observances of the Law.

Then when he says, **Behold, I Paul tell you,** he explains
these two parts of his admonition:

First, the second part;
Secondly, the first part (v. 5).

As to the first, he does two things:

First, he shows what the yoke of bondage is that they
  ought not submit to;
Secondly, he proves it (v. 4).

Regarding the first, he does two things:

First, he shows that this yoke is a source of great harm;
Secondly, that it is terribly burdensome (v. 3).

The yoke of the Law is harmful because it nullifies the
effect of the Lord's passion. Hence he says, **be not held again
under the yoke of bondage,** because **behold, I Paul,** who
am speaking with the voice of authority, **tell you,** and well,
**that if you be circumcised, Christ shall profit you nothing,**
i.e., faith in Christ.

But against this is something recorded in Acts (16:3),
namely, that Paul circumcised Timothy. Hence in effect he
brought it about that Christ profited him nothing; furthermore, he was deceiving him. I answer that, according to
Jerome, Paul did not circumcise Timothy as though intending
to observe the Law, but he feigned circumcision in working
circumcision on him. For, according to him, the apostles
feigned observing the works of the Law to avoid scandalizing the believers from Judaism. In other words, they performed the actions of the Law without the intention of
observing them, and so they departed not from the faith.
Hence he did not deceive Timothy.

However, according to Augustine, the answer is that the
apostles did in very truth observe the works of the Law and
had the intention of observing them; because, according to
the teaching of the apostles, it was lawful at that time, i.e.,

before grace had become widespread, for converts from Judaism to observe them. Therefore, because Timothy was born of a Jewish mother, the Apostle circumcised him with the intention of observing the Law. But because the Galatians were putting their hope in the legal observances after the spreading of grace, as though without them grace was not sufficient to save them, and they observed them in that frame of mind, for that reason the Apostle declared to them that **if you be circumcised, Christ shall profit you nothing.** For it followed from this that they did not correctly estimate Christ, to signify Whom circumcision was given: "That it may be a sign of the covenant between me and you" (Gen. 17:11). Therefore, those who submitted to circumcision believed that the sign was still in vogue and that the one signified had not yet come. Thus they were fallen away from Christ. In this way, then, it is plain that the yoke of the Law is harmful.

Furthermore, it is a heavy burden, because it obliges to the impossible. And this is what he states: **I testify again to every man circumcising himself, that he is a debtor to do the whole law.** As if to say: I say that **if you be circumcised, Christ shall profit you nothing.** But in addition to this, **I testify to every man,** both Jew and Gentile, **circumcising himself, that he is a debtor to do the whole law.** For one who professes a religion makes himself a debtor to all that pertains to the observances of that religion. And, as Augustine says: "There has never been a religion without some visible sign to which those who live in that religion are obligated; as in the Christian religion the visible sign is Baptism, which all Christians are held to undergo. Furthermore, they are obligated to everything that pertains to the Christian religion." Now the sign of the Mosaic Law was circumcision. Therefore, whoever circumcised himself was put under obligation to observe and fulfill all the matters of the Law. And that is what he says: **he is a debtor to do the whole law:** "Whosoever offends in one point, is become guilty of all"

(Jas. 2:10). No one, however, was able to keep the Law, according to Acts (15:10): "This is a yoke which neither our fathers nor we have been able to bear."

But suppose someone is circumcised; then according to the aforesaid he is obligated to observe all the matters of the Law. But this is to sin mortally. Therefore, he is obligated to sin mortally and thus he sins in either case.

I answer that on the assumption that the same conviction prevails, he is obliged to observe the matters of the Law: for example, if one is convinced that he would sin mortally unless he were circumcised, then, having become circumcised, if the same conviction remains, he would sin mortally were he not to observe the matters of the Law. The reason for this is that the conviction that something must be done is nothing else but a judgment that it would be against God's will not to do it. If this is the case, I say that unless he did what his convictions dictate, he would sin mortally, not by reason of the work done but by reason of his conscience. Likewise, if he does it, he sins, because ignorance of this kind does not excuse him, since he is ignorant of a precept. Nevertheless, he is not absolutely perplexed, but only in a qualified sense, because it is within his power to correct his erroneous conscience. And this is the way the Apostle is here testifying to everyone who circumcises himself that he is obliged to observe the ceremonies of the Law.

Then when he says, **You are made void of Christ,** he proves what he said, namely, that they must not embrace the observances of the Law, because it involves a double injury: first, the loss of Christ; secondly, the loss of grace. Moreover, the first is the cause of the second, because **you who are justified in the law are fallen from grace.**

He says therefore, **You are made void of Christ.** As if to say: Verily Christ will profit you nothing, because you are made void of Christ, i.e., of living in Christ. The second injury is the loss of grace. Hence he says: **you are fallen from grace,** i.e., you who were full of the grace of Christ, "because of his fulness we have all received" (Jn. 1:16); "The heart of a fool is like a broken vessel and no wisdom at all shall it hold" (Ecclus. 22:17). **You,** I say, **who are justified in the law,** i.e., who believe that you are justified, **are fallen**—"Be mindful, therefore, from whence thou art fallen and do penance" (Apoc. 2:5).—**from grace,** namely, from possessing future happiness or even from the grace you once had.

# CHAPTER 5

### LECTURE 2

5 For we in spirit, by faith, wait for the hope of justice.
6 For in Christ Jesus neither circumcision availeth any thing, nor uncircumcision; but faith that worketh by charity.
7 You did run well. Who hath hindered you, that you should not obey the truth?
8 This persuasion is not from him that calleth you.
9 A little leaven corrupteth the whole lump.
10 I have confidence in you in the Lord that you will not be of another mind; but he that troubleth you shall bear the judgment, whosoever he be.
11 And I, brethren, if I yet preach circumcision, why do I yet suffer persecution? Then is the scandal of the cross made void.
12 I would they were even cut off, who trouble you.

Having explained the second point, namely, that they must not submit to the yoke of serving the Law, the Apostle here returns to the first and shows that they must stand fast.

First, he gives an example of standing;
Secondly, he removes an obstacle to standing (v. 7);
Thirdly, he tells them its mode (v. 13).

As to the first, he does two things:

First, he proposes an example of standing;
Secondly, he assigns its cause (v. 6).

He says therefore: Those who want to be justified in the Law, Christ profits them nothing, because they are fallen from grace. But we, namely, the apostles, stand through hope, because **we wait for the hope of justice,** i.e., for justice and hope, namely, eternal happiness: "He hath regenerated us unto a lively hope by the resurrection of Jesus Christ from the dead" (1 Pet. 1:3). Or, **the hope of justice,** i.e., Christ, by Whom we have a hope for justice, because we are justified by Him: "We look for the savior, Our Lord Jesus Christ" (Phil. 3:20); "Who of God is made unto us wisdom and justice and sanctification and redemption" (1 Cor. 1:30). Or, **the hope of justice,** i.e., the hope which is concerned with justice; that we be justified not by the Law but by faith: "We account a man to be justified by faith without the works of the law" (Rom. 3:28). Or, **the hope of justice,** i.e., the things we hope for, and unto which justice tends, namely, eternal life: "As to the rest, there is laid up for me a crown of justice which the Lord, the just judge, will render to me in that day" (2 Tim. 4:8).

And this **by faith,** "because the justice of God is by faith of Jesus Christ," as is said in Romans (3:22). Which faith is not of man but of the Holy Spirit Who inspires it. "You have received the spirit of adoption of Sons, whereby we cry: Abba (Father)" (Rom. 8:15). Therefore, as faith is from the Spirit, so from faith is hope, and from hope the justice through which we reach eternal life. However, this hope does not come from circumcision or from paganism, because these contribute nothing to it. Hence he says, **For in Christ Jesus,** i.e., in those who live in the faith of Christ, **neither circumcision nor uncircumcision availeth anything,** i.e., they make no difference; **but faith,** not unformed, but the kind **that worketh by charity:** "Faith without works is dead" (Jas. 2:26). For faith is a knowledge of the word of God—"That Christ may dwell by faith in your hearts" (Eph. 3:17)—which word is not perfectly possessed or perfectly known unless the love which it hopes for is possessed.

Here a Gloss raises two problems. The first is that he says circumcision and uncircumcision to be indifferent, whereas above he had said, **If you be circumcised, Christ will profit you nothing.** I answer that it is from the general nature of the work that they are indifferent, namely, to those who do not put any trust in them; however, they are not indifferent, if you consider the intention of the one acting. For they are deadly to those who put their trust in them.

The second problem concerns his saying that those who do not believe are worse than demons, for the demons believe and tremble. I answer that if you consider the nature of the work, they are worse; but not if you consider the will. For the demons are displeased by the fact of their believing; furthermore, there is not as much malice in the will of a man who does not believe as there is in the demon who hates what he believes.

Then when he says, **You did run well. Who hath hindered you that you should not obey the truth?** he deals with the obstacle to standing.

First, he mentions the obstacle;
Secondly, he teaches its removal (v. 8).

The obstacle to their standing fast was great and harmful, for the harmfulness of anything is reckoned according to the greater good it hinders. Therefore, when someone is kept from many spiritual goods, it is an indication that he is faced with a great obstacle. Accordingly, in order to show them that they have a great obstacle, he reminds them of the spiritual goods they have lost, when he says: **You did run well,** namely, by means of the works of faith formed by charity, which incites one to run: "I have run the way of thy commandments, when thou didst enlarge my heart" (Ps. 118:32). And this did indeed apply to you formerly; but while you were thus running, you came upon an obstacle. Therefore he says: **Who hath bewitched you?** (This has been discussed already in Chapter 3, hence we pass over it now).

Therefore, who has bewitched you, i.e., **hindered the truth,** namely, of the Gospel, **that you should not obey it?** This is appropriately said: for obedience is the application of the will to the edict of the one who commands. That is why faith is a science of the will and of the understanding. It is suitable, therefore, for the will to obey the faith. But this is done by willing to believe that the grace of Christ is sufficient for salvation without the legal observances.

Then when he says, **Consent to no one** [not in Vulgate], he removes the obstacle.

First, on their part;
Secondly, on God's part (v. 10);
Thirdly, on the Apostle's part (v. 11).

On their part when he says, **Consent to no one.** Herein he shows what is required on their part to overcome this obstacle, namely, that henceforth they not give their consent to any deceiver: "We are not of the night nor of the darkness; therefore, let us not sleep" (1 Thess. 5:5); "Have no fellowship with the unfruitful works of darkness but rather reprove them" (Eph. 5:11); "And their speech spreadeth like a canker" (2 Tim. 2:17). From this it can be gathered that they were not yet corrupted, but he was concerned.

Secondly, he gives an explanation of this, when he says, **This persuasion is not from him that calleth you;** and it is twofold. First, because a man, when he gives himself to someone, ought to do nothing save what is of advantage to the latter. But you have been given to Christ. Therefore, you should not heed or consent to anyone but those who come from Him. Hence because **this persuasion,** by which they wish to set you under the yoke of the Law, **is not from him,** i.e., from God **who calleth you** to life, but from the devil, for it is degrading, you should not consent to them. Or, **not from him,** i.e., against Him.

The second explanation is that they might suppose that consenting to a few is not a great matter, since it constitutes no danger. But he says that they must not consent to them at all, nor underestimate their artifices; rather they must oppose them at the start, because **a little leaven corrupteth the whole lump,** i.e., those few who are persuading you. Or, **This persuasion** small in the beginning **corrupts the whole lump,** i.e., the congregation of the faithful: "Neither shall any leaven or honey be burnt in the sacrifice to the Lord" (Lev. 2:11).

Then when he says, **I have confidence in you in the Lord that you will not be of another mind,** he removes the obstacle on the part of God Who offers His help to this end. And he mentions a twofold help: one as to the deceivers; the other as to the trouble makers. He says therefore, **I have confidence in you in the Lord that you will not be of another mind.** As if to say: I have told you not to obey the deceivers and **I have confidence in you:** "I rejoice that in all things I have confidence in you" (2 Cor. 7:16); "But, dearly beloved, we trust better things of you and nearer to salvation" (Heb. 6:9). I have confidence, I say, in this, namely, **that you will not be of another mind** than what I have taught you—**but though we or an angel from heaven preach a Gospel to you besides that which we have preached to you, let him be anathema** (1:8); "Fulfill ye my joy, that you be of one mind" (Phil. 2:2)—and this with God's help. Hence he says, **in the Lord** God working: "And such confidence we have through Christ towards God" (2 Cor. 3:4), because the Lord will give you a mind according with the standard of the Catholic Faith: "It is good to have confidence in the Lord rather than to have confidence in a man" (Ps. 117:8).

As to the trouble makers, he says, **he that troubleth you shall bear the judgment, whosoever he be,** i.e., he that perverts you from right order so as to be turned from spiritual to corporeal things, whereas it should be the contrary: "Yet that was not first which was spiritual, but that which is natural; afterwards that which is spiritual" (1 Cor. 15:46).

Therefore, **he shall bear the judgment,** i.e., he will undergo damnation. For as one who urges another to good is rewarded—"They that instruct many to justice shall shine as stars for all eternity" (Dan. 12:3)—so one who urges another to evil is condemned: "Because thou hast troubled us, the Lord trouble thee this day" (Jos. 7:25); "Curst be he that maketh the blind to wander out of his way" (Deut. 27:18). And this, **whosoever he be,** i.e., whatever his dignity, he will not be spared.

But Porphyry and Julian censure Paul for presumption, and assert that in saying this he defames Peter (since he wrote above that he withstood him to his face) so that the meaning would be: **whosoever he be,** i.e., even if it be Peter, he would be punished. But as Augustine says, one should not believe that Paul was calling down a curse on the Prince of the Church—for it is written in Exodus (22:28): "Thou shalt not curse the prince of thy people"—or that Peter committed an offence worthy of damnation. Therefore the Apostle is speaking of someone else who, coming from Judea, claimed to be a disciple of the important apostles and with that authority he and other false teachers were subverting the Galatians, **because of false brethren unawares brought in** (2:4).

Then when he says, **And I brethren, if I yet preach circumcision, why do I yet suffer persecution?,** he removes the obstacle on his part.

> First, he presents his defense;
> Secondly, he rebukes his slanderers (v. 12).
>
> He refutes the false charge against him.
>
> First, a charge that pertains to himself alone;
> Secondly, one that pertains to all (v. 11).

With respect to the first, it should be noted that the false brethren, when the Galatians excused themselves from observing the legal ceremonies because they had been so taught by the Apostle, declared that the Apostle misled them and that he persuaded them to this in order to lord it over them. As confirmation of this they alleged that when he preached in Judea, Paul taught that the legal ceremonies should be observed. But the Apostle clears himself of this, when he says, **And I, brethren, if I yet preach circumcision, why do I yet suffer persecution** from the Jews? "We are persecuted and we suffer it" (1 Cor. 4:12). For the Jews persecuted Paul precisely because he taught that the legal ceremonies should not be observed. Indeed in Acts (21:21) James says to Paul: "They have heard of thee that thou teachest those Jews who are among the Gentiles to depart from Moses; saying that they ought not to circumcise their children nor walk according to custom." It is plain, therefore, that their charge is not true; otherwise, he would not have suffered their persecutions.

False, too, is that which they impute to me because of something generally held by others; because if I preach circumcision, **Then is the scandal of the cross made void.** For not only I but all the apostles "preach Christ crucified, to the Jews indeed a stumbling-block and unto the Gentiles, foolishness," as is said in 1 Corinthians (1:23). And the main reason why they are scandalized is because we preach that through the Cross of Christ the legal ceremonies are made void. Therefore, if I preach circumcision, the stumbling-block is removed, i.e., there will no longer be a stumbling-block for the Jews from the Cross. For they would endure it patiently; indeed, they would welcome it, if along with the Cross we preached the obligation to observe the legal ceremonies. Or, according to Augustine (on this passage) **the scandal of the cross is made void,** i.e., the Cross is made void; which is a scandal. As if to say: The Cross has lost its effect and its power: **If justice be by the law, then Christ died in vain** (2:21). Now the Apostle specifically says, **the scandal of the cross is made void,** to denote that the reason the Jews killed Christ was because He did not observe the legal ceremonies and taught that they were not to be observed: "This man is not of God who keepeth not the sabbath" (Jn. 9:16).

Then he rebukes the false brethren who had slandered him, saying, **I would they were even cut off who trouble you.** As if to say: They trouble you on one matter, namely, they want you to be circumcised; but I would that they be not only circumcised but wholly emasculated.

But this is contrary to Romans (12:14): "Bless, and curse not." To this there are two responses: first, that the Apostle was not calling down an evil on them but rather a blessing; because he was wishing them to be emasculated spiritually, i.e., abolish the legal ceremonies, that they might preserve spiritual chastity: "There are eunuchs who have made themselves such for the kingdom of heaven" (Mt. 19:12). The second is that he is wishing them the impotence that eunuchs have, so that they might not procreate. Hence he says: **I would they were even cut off who trouble you,** i.e., that they lose the power of engendering among you and others. And this deservedly, because they engender sons unto error and subject them to the bondage of the Law: "Give them a womb without children, and dry breasts" (Os. 9:14).

# CHAPTER 5

## Lecture 3

13 For you, brethren, have been called unto liberty. Only make not liberty an occasion to the flesh; but by charity of the spirit serve one another.
14 For all the law is fulfilled in one word: Thou shalt love thy neighbour as thyself.
15 But if you bite and devour one another; take heed you be not consumed one of another.

Having proposed an example of standing, and eliminated an obstacle thereto, he now establishes its mode.

First, he establishes the mode of standing;
Secondly, he gives an explanation (v. 14).

As to the first he does three things:

First, he sets down the condition of a state;
Secondly, he describes its abuse;
Thirdly, he asserts its mode (v. 13).

The condition of standing is liberty. For the condition
of any given state pertains either to liberty or to bondage;
but the state of faith in Christ, to which the Apostle urges
them, pertains to liberty and is liberty itself. Hence he says:
**For you, brethren, have been called unto liberty.** As if to
say: They are indeed troubling you; for they are drawing
you from what is better to what is worse, because **you have
been called** by God **unto the liberty** of grace: "You have not
received the spirit of bondage again in fear, but you have
received the spirit of adoption of sons" (Rom. 8:15); **We
are not the children of the bondwoman but of the free**
(4:31). You, I say, who are free in Christ, they want to lead
into bondage. But a state is being misused if it declines and
if liberty of the spirit is perverted into slavery of the flesh.
Now the Galatians were free of the Law; but lest they suppose this to be a license to commit sins forbidden by the
Law, the Apostle touches on abuse of liberty, saying, **Only
make not liberty an occasion to the flesh.** As if to say: You
are free, but not so as to misuse your liberty by supposing
that you may sin with impunity: "But take heed, lest perhaps this your liberty become a stumbling-block to the weak"
(1 Cor. 8:9).

Now the mode of standing is through charity; hence he
says: **but by charity of the spirit serve one another.** In fact
the whole state consists in charity, without which a man is
nothing (1 Cor. 13:1 ff.). Moreover, it is according to the
various degrees of charity that various states are distinguished.
Consequently, the state of grace does not exist in virtue of a
desire of the flesh but **by charity of the spirit,** i.e., a charity

which proceeds from the Holy Spirit, through Whom we should
be subject to and serve one another: **Bear ye one another's
burdens** (6:2); "With honor preventing one another" (Rom.
12:10).

But since he said earlier that they have been called
unto liberty, why does he now say, **serve one another?** I
answer that charity requires that we serve one another; nevertheless, it is free. Here one might interject that, as the Philosopher says, he is free who is for his own sake; whereas
he is a slave who is for the sake of another as of a mover
or an end. For a slave is moved to his work not by himself
but by a master and for the benefit of his master. Charity,
therefore, has liberty as to its movent cause, because it works
of itself: "The charity of Christ presseth us" spontaneously,
to work (2 Cor. 5:14). But it is a servant when, putting one's
own interests aside, it devotes itself to things beneficial to
the neighbor.

Then when he says, **For all the law is fulfilled in one
word,** he explains what he says:

First, about charity;
Secondly, about not making liberty an occasion to the
   flesh (v. 16).

As to the first he admonishes them to follow charity:

First, because of the benefit we obtain in fulfilling charity;
Secondly, because of the injury incurred by neglecting
   charity (v. 15).

Now the benefit we obtain in fulfilling charity is of the
highest order, because in it we fulfill the whole law; hence
he says, **For all the law in fulfilled in one word.** As if to say:
Charity must be maintained, because the whole law is fulfilled in one word, namely, in the one precept of charity: "He
that loveth his neighbor hath fulfilled the law" (Rom. 13:8)
and "Love is the fulfillment of the law" (13:10). Wherefore

he says in 1 Timothy (1:5): "The end of the commandment is charity."

However, it is said in Matthew (22:40): "On these two commandments," namely, of the love of God and of neighbor, "dependeth the whole law and the prophets." Therefore, it is not fulfilled in the one precept alone. I answer that in the love of God is included love of neighbor: "This commandment we have from God, that he, who loveth God, love also his brother" (1 Jn. 4:21). Conversely, we love our neighbor for the love of God. Consequently, the whole law is fulfilled in the one precept of charity. For the precepts of the law are reduced to that one precept. Indeed, precepts are either moral or ceremonial or judicial. The moral are the precepts of the decalogue: three concern the love of God, and the other seven the love of neighbor. The judicial are, for example, that whosoever steals anything shall restore fourfold, and others like this; and they pertain absolutely to the love of neighbor. The ceremonial concern sacrifices and related matters which are reduced to love of God. And so it is plain that all are fulfilled in the one precept of charity, **Thou shalt love thy neighbor as thyself**, which is also written in Leviticus (19:18).

He says, **as thyself**, not "as much as thyself," because according to the order of charity a man should love himself more than his neighbor. Now this is explained in three ways: First, as referring to the genuineness of the love. For to love is to will good to someone: hence we are said to love both the one to whom we will a good and the very good which we will to someone; but not in the same way. For when I will a good to myself, I love myself absolutely for myself, but the good which I will to myself, I do not love for itself but for myself. Accordingly, I love my neighbor as myself in the same way that I love myself, when I will him a good for his sake, and not because it is useful or pleasant for me. In a second way, as referring to the justice of love. For each thing is inclined to want for itself that which is most eminent in it; but in man, understanding and reason are the most eminent. He, therefore, loves himself who wants for himself the good of understanding and reason. Accordingly, you then love your neighbor as yourself, when you will him the good of understanding and reason. In a third way, as referring to order, i.e., that just as you love yourself for the sake of God, so you love your neighbor for the sake of God, namely, that he may attain to God.

Then when he says, **But if you bite and devour one another, take heed you be not consumed one of another,** he urges them to follow charity, because of the harm we incur if we neglect it. Here he continues to speak to the Galatians as to spiritual men, not bringing up their greater vices but mentioning ones that seem to be minor, such as sins of the tongue. Hence he says: **If you bite and devour one another, take heed you be not consumed one of another.** As if to say: All the law is fulfilled in love; **but if you bite one another,** i.e., partially destroy the good name of your neighbor by slander (for one who bites takes not the whole but a part) **and devour,** i.e., destroy his good name entirely, and completely shame him by slander (for he that devours, consumes all): "Detract not one another, my brethren; he that detracteth his brother detracteth the law" (Jas. 4:11). If you neglect charity in that way, I say, **take heed** for the calamity that threatens you, namely, **you might be devoured one of another:** "Beware of dogs, beware of evil workers, beware of the concision" (Phil. 3:2); "I have spent my strength without cause and in vain" (Is. 49:4). For as Augustine says, by the vice of contention and envy pernicious rivalries are bred among men, and both life and society are thereby brought to ruin.

# CHAPTER 5

## LECTURE 4

16 I say then: Walk in the spirit; and you shall not fulfil the lusts of the flesh.

17 For the flesh lusteth against the spirit; and the spirit against the flesh. For these are contrary one to another; so that you do not the things that you would.

After indicating what the spiritual state consists in, namely, in charity, the Apostle then deals with the cause of the state, namely, of the Holy Spirit Whom he says they must follow. And he mentions three benefits obtained from the Holy Spirit.

First, freedom from the bondage of the flesh;
Secondly, freedom from the bondage of the Law (v. 18);
Thirdly, the conferring of life, or security from the damnation of death (v. 25).

As to the first, he does two things:

First, he sets down the first benefit of the spirit;
Secondly, he shows the need for this benefit (v. 17).

He says therefore: I say that you are obliged by charity of spirit to serve one another, because nothing profits without charity. But this **I say in Christ** [not in Vulgate], i.e., by the faith of Christ, **walk in the spirit,** i.e., in the mind and reason. For sometimes our mind is called a spirit, according to Ephesians (4:23): "Be renewed in the spirit of your mind," and "I will sing with the spirit, I will sing also with the understanding" (1 Cor. 14:15). Or, **walk in the spirit,** i.e., make progress in the Holy Spirit, by acting well. For the Holy Spirit moves and incites hearts to do well: "Whoso-

ever are led by the Spirit of God, they are the sons of God"
(Rom. 8:14). One should walk, therefore, by the spirit, i.e.,
the mind, so that one's reason or mind is in accord with the
Law of God, as it is said in Romans (7:16). For the human
spirit is fickle, and unless it is governed from elsewhere, it
turns now in one direction and now in another, as is said in
Ecclesiasticus (34:6): "The heart fancieth as that of a woman
in travail. Except it be a vision sent forth from the most High,
set not thy heart upon them." Hence Ephesians (4:17) says
of certain ones: "They walk in the vanity of their mind."
Therefore the human reason cannot stand perfectly except to
the extent that it is governed by a divine spirit.

Accordingly the Apostle says, **walk in the spirit,** i.e.,
under the rule and guidance of the Holy Spirit, Whom we
should follow as one pointing out the way. For knowledge
of the supernatural end is in us only from the Holy Spirit:
"Eye hath not seen nor ear heard, neither hath it entered
into the heart of man what things God hath prepared for
them that love Him," and immediately is added, "But to us
God hath revealed them by his Spirit" (1 Cor. 2:9). Also as
one who inclines us. For the Holy Spirit stirs up and turns
the affections to right willing: "Whosoever are led by the
Spirit of God, they are the sons of God" (Rom. 8:14); "Thy
good spirit shall lead me into the right land" (Ps. 142:10).

Now one ought to walk in the spirit, because it frees
him from the defilement of the flesh. Hence he follows with:
**and you shall not fulfil the lusts of the flesh,** i.e., the pleasures which the flesh suggests. This the Apostle yearned for,
saying: "Unhappy man that I am, who shall deliver me from
the body of this death?" (Rom. 7:24). Later he concludes:
"There is now therefore no condemnation to them that are
in Christ Jesus, who walk not according to the flesh" (Rom.
8:1). And at once he gives the reason for this: "For the law
of the spirit of life in Christ Jesus hath delivered me from
the law of sin and of death" (Rom. 8:2). And this is the
special desire of the saints, that they not fulfill the desires

to which the flesh stirs them, but always understanding that in this are not included desires which pertain to the necessities of the flesh, but those that pertain to superfluities.

Then when he says, **For the flesh lusteth against the spirit,** he tells why this benefit is needed, namely, because of the struggle between flesh and spirit.

First, he asserts that there is a struggle;
Secondly, he elucidates this by an obvious sign (v. 17).

He says therefore: It is necessary that by the spirit you overcome the desires of the flesh, **for the flesh lusteth against the spirit.** But one might have a doubt here, because, since lusting is an act of the soul alone, it does not seem to come from the flesh. I answer that, according to Augustine, the flesh is said to lust inasmuch as the soul lusts by means of the flesh, just as the eye is said to see, when as a matter of fact, it is the soul that sees by means of the eye. Consequently, the soul lusts by means of the flesh, when it seeks, according to the flesh, things which are pleasurable. But the soul lusts by means of itself, when it takes pleasure in things that are according to the spirit, as virtuous works, contemplation of divine things, and mediation of wisdom: "The desire of wisdom bringeth to the everlasting kingdom" (Wis. 6:21).

But if the flesh lusts by means of the spirit, how does it lust against it? It does so in the sense that the lusting of the flesh hinders the desires of the spirit. For since the pleasures of the flesh concern goods which are beneath us, whereas the pleasures of the spirit concern goods which are above us, it comes to pass that when the soul is occupied with the lower things of the flesh, it is withdrawn from the higher things of the spirit.

But his further statement that **the spirit lusts against the flesh** may cause a problem. For if we take "spirit" for the Holy Spirit, and the desire of the Holy Spirit is against evil things, it seems to follow that the flesh against which the spirit lusts is evil—which is the Manichean error. I answer that the spirit does not lust against the nature of the flesh, but against its desires, namely, those that concern super-fluities; hence he said above, **you shall not fulfil the lusts of the flesh** (v. 16), i.e., superflous things. For in things nec-essary the spirit does not contradict the flesh, as we are told in Ephesians (5:29): "No man hateth his own flesh."

Then when he says, **For these are contrary one to an-other,** he gives evidence of the struggle. As if to say: It is obvious from experience that they fight and struggle against one another, so far forth **that you do not,** i.e., are not suffered to do, **the things,** good or evil, **that you would:** "The good which I will I do not: but the evil which I will not, that I do" (Rom. 7:19). However, free will is not taken away. For since free will consists in having choice, there is free-dom of the will with respect to things subject to choice. But not all that lies in us is fully subject to our choice, but only in a qualified sense. In specific cases we are able to avoid this or that movement of lust or anger, but we can-not avoid all movements of anger or lust in general—and this by reason of the "fomes" introduced by the first sin.

Here it should be noted that with respect to lusts there are four categories of men who do not that which they would. For intemperate men, who of set intention follow the pas-sions of the flesh—according to Proverbs (2:14): "They are glad when they have done evil"—do, indeed, what they will, inasmuch as they follow their passions; but inasmuch as their reason complains and is displeased, they are doing what they would not. But incontinent persons, who resolve to abstain but are, nevertheless, conquered by their passions, do what they would not, inasmuch as they follow such passions con-trary to what they resolved. As between these two types the intemperate do more of the things that they would. Those, however, who are continent, i.e., who would prefer not to lust at all, do what they intend, as long as they are not subject to lust; but because they cannot completely repress lust, they do what they would not. Finally, those who are temperate do what they would, inasmuch as there is no lust in the tamed flesh; but because it cannot be totally tamed so as never to rise up against the spirit—just as neither can malice so abound that reason would never complain—therefore, in those instances in which they do lust, they are doing what they would not; but for the most part they do what they would.

# CHAPTER 5

## LECTURE 5

18 But if you are led by the spirit, you are not under the law.
19 Now the works of the flesh are manifest, which are: fornication, uncleanness, immodesty, luxury,
20 Idolatry, witchcrafts, enmities, contentions, emulations, wraths, quarrels, dissension, sects,
21 Envies, murders, drunkenness, revellings, and such like. Of the which I foretell you, as I have foretold to you, that they who do such things shall not obtain the kingdom of God.

After showing that through the spirit we are freed from the desires of the flesh, the Apostle here shows that through it we are released from the bondage of the Law.

First, he mentions a benefit of the spirit;
Secondly, he manifests it by certain effects (v. 19).

He says therefore: I say that if you walk in the spirit, not only will you not carry out the desires of the flesh, but, what is more, **if you are led by the spirit** (which happens when you do what the spirit suggests, as director and guide, and not what your sense desires urge, **you are not under the** law: "Thy good spirit shall lead me into the right land," not by compelling, but by guiding (Ps. 142:10).

Jerome infers from these words that after the coming of Christ no one having the Holy Spirit is obliged to observe the Law. But it should be recognized that the saying, **if you are led by the spirit, you are not under the law,** can be referred either to the ceremonial or to the moral precepts of the Law. If it is referred to the ceremonial precepts, then it is one thing to observe the Law and another to be under the Law. For to observe the Law is to carry out the works of the Law without putting any hope in them; but to be under the Law is to put one's hope in the works of the Law. Now in the early Church there were some just men who observed the Law without being under the Law, inasmuch as they observed the works of the Law; but they were not under the Law in the sense of putting their hope in them. In this way even Christ was under the Law: **Made under the law** (4:4). Thus Jerome's opinion is excluded.

But if it is referred to the moral precepts, then to be under the Law can be taken in two ways: either as to its obliging force, and then all the faithful are under the Law, because it was given to all—hence it is said: "I have not come to destroy the law but to fulfill it" (Mt. 5:17)—or as to its compelling forces, and then the just are not under the Law, because the movements and breathings of the Holy Spirit in them are their inspiration; for charity inclines to the very things that the Law prescribes. Therefore, because the just have an inward law, they willingly do what the Law commands and are not constrained by it. But those who would do evil but are held back by a sense of shame or by fear of the Law are compelled. Accordingly, the just are under the Law as obliging but not as compelling, in which sense the unjust alone are under it: "Where the spirit of the Lord is, there is liberty" (2 Cor. 3:17); "The law," as compelling, "is not made for the just man" (1 Tim. 1:9).

Then when he says, **the works of the flesh are manifest,**
he proves what he has said through certain effects.

> First, he mentions the works of the flesh which are op-
>    posed to the Holy Spirit;
> Secondly, he shows how the works of the Spirit are not
>    forbidden by the Law (23b).

As to the first, he does two things:

> First, he mentions the works of the flesh that are for-
>    bidden by the Law;
> Secondly, the works of the Spirit which are not for-
>    bidden by it (v. 22).

As to the first, he does two things:

> First, he enumerates the works of the flesh;
> Secondly, he mentions the harm that follows from them
>    (v. 21).

With respect to the first, two doubts arise. First, as to
the Apostle's mentioning things that do not pertain to the
flesh, but which he says are works of the flesh, such as
idolatry, sects, emulations, and the like. I answer that, according to Augustine in *The City of God,* (Bk. 14), he lives
according to the flesh who lives according to himself. Hence
flesh is taken here as referring to the whole man. Accordingly,
whatever springs from disordered self-love is called a work
of the flesh. Or, one should say that a sin can be called "of
the flesh" in two ways: namely, with respect to fulfillment,
and in this sense only those are sins of the flesh that are
fulfilled in the pleasure of the flesh, namely, lust and glut-
tony; or with respect to their root, and in this sense all sins
are called sins of the flesh, inasmuch as the soul is so weighed
down by the weakness of the flesh (as is written in Wisdom
9:15) that the enfeebled intellect can be easily misled and
hindered from operating perfectly. As a consequence, certain vices follow therefrom, namely, heresies, sects and the

like. In this way it is said that the "fomes" is the source of all sins.

The second doubt is that, since the Apostle says that **they who do such things shall not obtain the kingdom of God,** whereas no one is excluded from the kingdom of God except for mortal sin, it follows that all the sins enumerated are mortal sins. But the contrary seems to be the case, because in this list he enumerates many that are not mortal sins, such as contention, emulation, and the like. I answer that all the sins listed here are mortal one way or another: some are so according to their genus, as murder, fornication, idolatry, and the like; but others are mortal with respect to fulfillment, as anger, whose fulfillment consists in harm to neighbor. Hence if one consents to that harm, there is mortal sin. In like manner, eating is directed to the pleasure of food, but if one places his end in such pleasures, he sins mortally; accordingly, he does not say "eating" but **revellings.** And the same must be said of the others that are like this.

Thirdly, there is a doubt about the order followed in this list. However, it should be recognized that when the Apostle varies his enumeration of various vices in various texts, it is not his intention to enumerate all the vices in perfect order and according to the rules of the art, but only those in which the persons to whom he is writing abound and in which they are excessive. Therefore in these lists one should look not for completeness but for the cause of the variation.

Having settled these doubts, we should next observe that the Apostle lists certain vices of the flesh that concern things not necessary to life and others that concern things necessary to life. As to the first, he mentions certain vices that a man commits against himself; then those that are against God; finally, those that are against the neighbor.

Against the self are four. These he mentions first, because they obviously spring from the flesh. Two of these pertain to the carnal act of lust, namely, **fornication,** when an unmarried man becomes one with an unmarried woman with respect to the natural use of lust. The other is **uncleanness** as to a use which is contrary to nature—"No fornicator or unclean . . . hath inheritance in the kingdom of Christ and of God" (Eph. 5:5); "They have not done penance for the uncleanness and fornication and lasciviousness that they have committed" (2 Cor. 12:21). The other two are ordained to the aforesaid acts: one is performed outwardly, as touches, looks, kisses and the like; as to these he says, **immodesty**: "Who despairing, have given themselves up to immodesty unto the working of all uncleanness" (Eph. 4:19). The other inwardly, namely, unclean thoughts; as to this he says, **luxury**: "When they have grown wanton in Christ, they will marry" (1 Tim. 5:11).

Against God he lists two: one of these is that whereby divine worship is hindered by the enemies of God; as to this he says, **idolatry**: "Neither become ye idolaters as some of them" (1 Cor. 10:7); "For the worship of abominable idols is the cause and beginning and end of all evil" (Wis. 14:27). The other is that in which a pact is struck with demons; as to this he says, **witchcrafts**, which are performed through magical arts, and are called in Latin *veneficia,* from venom, because they result in great harm to man: "I would not that you should be made partakers with devils" (1 Cor. 10:20); "Without are dogs and sorcerers" (Apoc. 22:15).

Against one's neighbor he enumerates nine, the first of which is **enmity** and the last **murder,** because from the former, one comes to the latter. The first, therefore, is animosity in the heart, which is hatred toward one's neighbor: "And a man's enemies shall be they of his own household" (Mt. 10:36); hence he says **enmities**: from which arise verbal disputes. And so he says, **contentions**, which are attacks on the truth with the confidence of shouting: "It is an honor for a man to separate himself from quarrels" (Prov. 20:3).

The second is **emulation**, which consists in contending with another to obtain a same thing; hence he says, **emula-**

tions, which arise from contention. The third arises when one is hindered by someone else who is tending to a same thing, so that on this account anger arises against him. Hence he says, **wraths:** "The anger of men worketh not the justice of God" (Jas. 1:20); "Let not the sun go down on your anger" (Eph. 4:26).

The fourth is when anger of spirit leads to blows; and with respect to this he says, **quarrels:** "Hatred stirs up strifes" (Prov. 10:12). The fifth, namely, **dissensions,** arise from quarrels: if they concern human matters they are called dissensions: for example, when factions arise in the Church—"Mark them who make dissensions and offences contrary to the doctrine which you have learned, and avoid them" (Rom. 16:17) —if they concern divine matters, they are called **sects,** i.e., heresies: "They shall bring in sects of perdition, and deny the Lord who bought them," and "They fear not to bring in sects, blaspheming" (2 Pet. 2:1, 10). From these **envy** follows, when those they vie with prosper: "Envy slayeth the little one" (Job 5:2). And from these follow **murders** in heart and deed: "Whosoever hateth his brother is a murderer" (1 Jn. 3:15).

Finally, of vices that pertain to the ordering of the necessaries of life he mentions two: one concerns drink; hence he says, **drunkenness,** i.e., continual: "Take heed lest perhaps your hearts be overcharged with surfeiting and drunkenness and the cares of this life" (Lk. 21:34). The other concerns food, touching which he says, **revellings:** "Not in rioting and drunkenness" (Rom. 13:13).

# CHAPTER 5

## LECTURE 6

22 But the fruit of the Spirit is: charity, joy, peace, patience, benignity, goodness, longanimity,
23a Mildness, faith, modesty, continency, chastity.

Having listed the works of the flesh, the Apostle then manifests the works of the spirit.

First, he manifests them;
Secondly, he shows how the Law is related to the works of the spirit and to the works of the flesh (v. 23b).

As to the first, he enumerates the spiritual goods which he calls "fruits." But here a question arises, because fruit is something we enjoy; but we should enjoy not our acts, but God alone. Therefore, acts of this kind, which the Apostle lists here, ought not be called "fruits." Furthermore, a Gloss says that these works of the spirit are to be sought for themselves; but that which is sought for itself is not referred to something else. Therefore virtues and their works are not to be referred to happiness.

I answer that "fruit" is said in two ways: namely, as something acquired, for example, from labor or study—"The fruit of good labors is glorious" (Wis. 3:15)—and as something produced, as fruit is produced from a tree: "A good tree cannot bear evil fruit" (Mt. 7:18). Now the works of the spirit are called fruits, not as something earned or acquired, but as produced. Furthermore, fruit which is acquired has the character of an ultimate end; not, however, fruit which is produced. Nevertheless, fruit so understood implies two things: namely, that it is the last thing of the producer, as the last thing produced by a tree is its fruit, and that it is sweet or delightful: "His fruit was sweet to my palate" (Cant. 2:3). So, then, the works of the virtues and of the spirit are something last in us. For the Holy Spirit is in us through grace, through which we acquire the habit of the virtues; these in turn make us capable of working according to virtue. Furthermore, they are delightful and even fruitful: "You have your fruit unto sanctification," i.e., in holy works (Rom. 6:22). And that is why they are called fruits. But they are also called "flowers," namely, in relation to future happiness; because just as from flowers hope of fruit is taken, so from works of the virtues is obtained hope of eternal life and happiness. And as in the flower there is a beginning of the fruit, so in the works of the virtues is a beginning of happiness, which will exist when knowledge and charity are made perfect.

From this the answer to the second objection is plain. For something can be said to be worthy of being sought *for* itself in two ways, according as "for" (*propter*) designates formal cause or final cause. Works of the virtues are to be sought for themselves formally but not finally, because they are a delight in themselves. For a sweet medicine is formally sought for itself, because it has something within itself that makes it pleasant, namely, sweetness, which however is sought for an end, namely, for the sake of health. But a bitter medicine is not sought formally for itself, because it does not please by reason of its form; yet it is sought for something else finally, namely, for health, which is its end.

This explains why the Apostle calls the effects of the flesh "works," but the fruits of the spirit he calls "fruits." For it has been pointed out that a fruit is something last and sweet, produced from a thing. On the other hand, that which is produced from something but not according to nature, does not have the character of fruit but is, as it were, an alien growth. Now the works of the flesh and sins are alien to the nature of those things which God has planted in our nature. For God planted in human nature certain seeds, namely, a natural desire of good and knowledge, and He added gifts of grace. And therefore, because the works of the virtues are produced naturally from these, they are called "fruits," but the works of the flesh are not. And for this reason, the Apostle says: "What fruit, therefore, had you then in those things of which you are now ashamed?" (Rom. 6:21). It is plain, therefore, from what has been said, that the works of the virtues are called fruits of the spirit, both because they have a sweetness and delight in themselves and because they are the last and congruous products of the gifts.

The difference from one another of the gifts, beatitudes, virtues and fruits is taken in the following way. In a virtue

can be considered the habit and the act. Now the habit of
a virtue qualifies a person to act well. If it enables him to
act well in a human mode, it is called a virtue. But if it qualifies one for acting well, above the human mode, it is called
a gift. Hence the Philosopher, above the common virtues, puts
certain heroic virtues: thus, to know the invisible things of
God darkly is in keeping with the human mode, and such
knowledge pertains to the virtue of faith; but to know the
same things more penetratingly and above the human mode
pertains to the gift of understanding. But as to the act of a
virtue, it is either perfective, and in this way is a beatitude;
or it is a source of delight, and in this way it is a fruit. Of
these fruits it is said in the Apocalypse (22:2): "On both
sides of the river was the tree of life, bearing twelve fruits."

He says, therefore, **the fruit of the Spirit,** which arises
in the soul from the sowing of spiritual grace, is **charity,
joy, peace, patience, longanimity** . . . which indeed are thus
distinguished because fruits perfect one either inwardly or
outwardly.

> First, he mentions those that perfect inwardly;
> Secondly, those that perfect outwardly (v. 22).

Now a man is perfected and directed inwardly both as
to good things and as to evil: "By the armor of justice on
the right hand and on the left" (2 Cor. 6:7). With respect
to good things a person is perfected, first of all, in his heart
through love. For just as in natural movements there is first
an inclination of a nature's appetite to its end, so the first of
the inward movements is the inclination to good, i.e., love;
accordingly, the first fruit is **charity:** "The charity of God is
poured forth in our hearts by the Holy Ghost Who is given
to us" (Rom. 5:5). And through charity the others are perfected; wherefore, the Apostle says in Colossians (3:14):
"But above all these things have charity, which is the bond
of perfection." But the ultimate end that perfects man in-

wardly is joy, which proceeds from the presence of the thing loved. And he that has charity already has what he loves: "He that abideth in charity abideth in God and God in him" (1 Jn. 4:16). And from this springs joy: "Rejoice in the Lord always; again I say, rejoice" (Phil. 4:4).

But this joy should be perfect, and for this two things are required: first, that the object loved be enough to perfect the lover. And as to this he says, **peace**. For it is then that the lover has peace, when he adequately possesses the object loved: "I am become in his presence as one finding peace" (Cant. 8:10). Secondly, that there be perfect enjoyment of the thing loved, which is likewise obtained by peace, because whatever else happens, if someone perfectly enjoys the object loved, say God, he cannot be hindered from enjoying it: "Much peace have they that love thy law and to them there is no stumbling-block" (Ps. 118:165). In this way, therefore, joy connotes the fruition of charity, but peace the perfection of charity. And by these is man inwardly made perfect as to good things.

Also with respect to evils, the Holy Spirit perfects and adjusts a person: first, against the evil that disturbs peace, which is disturbed by adverse objects. Touching this the Holy Spirit perfects one by patience, which makes for patient endurance of adversities; hence he says, **patience**: "In your patience you shall possess your souls" (Lk. 21:19). Secondly, against the evil which hinders joy, namely, the deferment of the object loved, the Spirit opposes long-suffering, which is not broken by delay. As to this he says, **longanimity**: "If it make any delay, wait for it; for it shall surely come, and it shall not be slack" (Hab. 2:3): "In long-suffering" (2 Cor. 6:6). Hence the Lord says in Matthew (10:22): "He that shall persevere unto the end, he shall be saved."

Then when he says, **goodness, benignity, . . .** he mentions the fruits of the spirit that perfect a man with respect to external things. Now external to man are things next to him, above him and beneath him. Next to him is the neighbor; above him is God; beneath him is his sensitive nature and body.

In regard to his neighbor He perfects men, first of all, from the heart with a right and good will. Concerning this he says, **goodness,** i.e., rectitude and gentleness of spirit. For if a man has all his other powers good, he cannot be said to be good unless he has a good will, according to which he uses all the others well. The reason for this is that the good denotes something perfect. But perfection is twofold: the first concerns the being of a thing; the second, its operation—and the latter is greater than the former. For that is called perfect in the absolute sense which has attained its perfect operation, which is its second perfection. Therefore, since it is by his will that man exercises the act of any power, right will makes for the good use of all the powers, and, consequently, makes the man himself good. Of this fruit it is said in Ephesians (5:9): "The fruit of the light is in all goodness and justice and truth." Secondly, He perfects a man in his deeds, so that he will share with his neighbor. Concerning this he says, **benignity,** i.e., giving: "The Lord loveth a cheerful giver" (2 Cor. 9:7). For benignity is said to be, as it were, a good fire, which makes a man melt to relieve the needs of others: "For the spirit of wisdom is benevolent" (Wis. 1:6); "Put ye on, therefore, as the elect of God, holy and beloved, the bowels of mercy, benignity . . ." (Coloss. 3:12). Again, they perfect one with respect to evils inflicted by others, so that one meekly bears and endures harassment from another. Touching this he says, **mildness:** "Learn of me, because I am meek and humble of heart" (Mt. 2:29); "To the meek he will give grace" (Prov. 3:34).

With respect to what is above us, namely, God, the Spirit establishes right order through faith; hence he says, **faith,** which is a knowledge of invisible things with certainty: "Abraham believed God and it was reputed to him unto justice" (Gen. 15:6); "He that cometh to God must believe that he is" (Heb. 11:6). On this account it is said in Ecclesiasticus

(1:34): "That which is agreeable to the Lord is faith and meekness."

Touching what is beneath us, namely, the body, the Spirit directs us first as to the outward acts of the body by modesty, which moderates its deeds or utterances—concerning this he says, **modesty**: "Let your modesty be known to all men" (Phil. 4:5). Secondly, as to the interior appetite, and concerning this he says **continency**, which abstains even from things that are lawful; and **chastity**, which correctly uses what is lawful, as a Gloss says. Or, another way: continence refers to the fact that although a man be assailed by base desires, yet by the vigor of his reason he holds fast lest he be carried away. According to this the word "continence" is taken from a person's holding fast under attack. But "chastity" is taken from the fact that one is neither attacked nor carried away, and is derived from "chastening." For we call him well-chastened who is rightly tempered in all things.

Concerning the aforesaid, two problems arise. The first is that since the fruits of the spirit are opposed to the works of the flesh, it seems that the Apostle should have mentioned as many fruits of the spirit as he mentioned works of the flesh—which he did not do. I answer that he did not do so, because there are more vices than virtues.

The second problem is that the fruits of the spirit mentioned do not correspond to the works of the flesh. I answer that since it is not the Apostle's intention here to teach the art of the virtues and vices, he does not set one against the other; but he mentions as many of the one and as many of the other as are suited to his present objective.

Yet a more diligent consideration discloses that they are in some fashion set in opposition. For in opposition to **fornication**, which is illicit love, is set **charity**; in opposition to **uncleanness, immodesty, and luxury**, which are allurements of the flesh that arise from fornication, is set **joy**, which is the spiritual delight produced by charity, as has been said. In opposition to what are called **witchcrafts, enmities, con-**

tentions, . . . dissensions, are set **patience, longanimity,** and **goodness.** To what are called **sects, faith** is set in opposition. To what is called **murder, benignity.** To what are called **drunkenness, revellings,** and the like, are opposed **modesty, continency** and **chastity.**

# CHAPTER 5

## LECTURE 7

23b Against such there is no law.
24 And they that are Christ's have crucified their flesh, with the vices and concupiscences.
25 If we live in the Spirit, let us also walk in the Spirit.
26 Let us not be made desirous of vainglory, provoking one another, envying one another.

Having enumerated the works of the flesh and of the spirit, the Apostle then concludes from both, that those who follow the spirit are not under the Law. The proof he uses is this: he is under the Law who is liable to the Law, i.e., who does things contrary to the Law. But those who are led by the spirit do not the works contrary to the Law. Therefore, they are not under the Law.

First, therefore, he proves the proposition on the part of
the works of the spirit;
Secondly, on the part of the works of the flesh (v. 24).

He says, therefore: I say that those who are led by the Spirit do not the works that are contrary to the Law, because they either do the works of the spirit, and **Against such there is no law,** i.e., against the works of the spirit, but the Spirit teaches such works. For as the Law outwardly teaches works of virtue, so the Spirit inwardly moves one to them: "For I am delighted with the law of God according to the inward man" (Rom. 7:22). Or they do the works of the flesh; and in those who are led by the spirit, such works are not contrary to the Law. Hence he says, **they that are Christ's,** i.e., who have the spirit of God; for "if any man have not the spirit of Christ, he is none of His" (Rom. 8:9). Accordingly, those are led by the spirit of God who are Christ's.

**They, I say, have crucified their flesh with the vices and concupiscences.** He does not say that they shun vices and concupiscences, because a good physician cures well, when he applies remedies against the cause of the disease. But the flesh is the root of vices. Therefore, if we would shun vices, the flesh must be tamed: "I chastise my body and bring it under subjection" (1 Cor. 9:27). But because the flesh is tamed by vigils, fasts and labors—"Torture and fetters are for a malicious slave; send him to work that he be not idle" (Ecclus. 33:28)—and one is led to such works out of devotion to Christ crucified. Therefore he specifically says, **they have crucified,** i.e., conformed themselves to Christ crucified by afflicting their flesh: "Our old man is crucified with him that the body of sin may be destroyed" (Rom. 6:6); **that I may live to God: with Christ I am nailed to the cross** (2:19).

But because they do not crucify the flesh by destroying nature, for "no one hates his own flesh" (Eph. 5:29), but with respect to matters that are contrary to the Law, for that reason he says, **with the vices,** i.e., with the sins, **and concupiscences,** i.e., passions, whereby the soul is inclined to sin. For he does not crucify his flesh well who leaves room for passions; otherwise, since reason is not always alert to avoid sin, as it ought, he might fall at some time: "Go not after thy lusts, but turn away from thy own will" (Ecclus. 18:30); "Make not provision for the flesh in its concupiscence" (Rom. 13:14).

Then when he says, **If we live in the Spirit, let us also walk in the Spirit,** he mentions the third benefit of the Holy Spirit, namely, the conferring of life.

First, he mentions this benefit of the Spirit of God;
Secondly, he rejects the vices of the spirit of the world
  (v. 26).

Therefore, including himself with those to whom he
writes, he says: I say that we ought to walk by the Spirit,
because we live by Him and not by the flesh: "We are
debtors not to the flesh to live according to the flesh" (Rom.
8:12). Therefore, **If we live in the Spirit,** we ought in all
things to be led by Him. For as in bodily life the body is
not moved save by the soul, by which it has life, so in the
spiritual life, all of our movements should be through the
Holy Spirit: "It is the spirit that giveth life" (Jn. 6:64); "In
him we live and move and are" (Ac. 17:28). But lest the
things said of the spirit be understood of the spirit of the
world—concerning which it is said in 1 Corinthians (2:12):
"We have received not the spirit of this world"—the Apostle
forestalls this when he says, **Let us not be made desirous of
vainglory, provoking one another, envying one another.** Here
he excludes things proper to the spirit of the world, namely,
vainglory, anger and envy, all three of which are aptly described by the word "spirit."

For "spirit" denotes a swelling. According to this, then,
those are called vain spirits who are swollen with vainglory:
"The blast of the mighty is like a whirlwind beating against
a wall" (Is. 25:4). Concerning this he says, **Let us not be
made desirous of vainglory,** i.e., of worldly glory. For since
that is vain which is not solidly established nor supported
by truth nor loved for any usefulness, then the glory of this
world is vain, because it is frail and not solid: "All flesh is
grass" (Is. 40:6). Furthermore, it is false—"The glory of
a sinful man is dung and worms" (1 Mac. 2:62)—whereas
true glory concerns goods appropriate to man, i.e., the goods
of the spirit, such as holy men have: "Our glory is this, the
testimony of our conscience" (2 Cor. 1:12). Furthermore,
this glory is useless and fruitless: for how great soever the
glory one acquires from the testimony of men, he cannot on

that account achieve his end, which is achieved by the testimony of God: "He that glorieth, let him glory in the Lord" (1 Cor. 1:31).

He does not say, "Do not have vainglory," but **be not made desirous of vainglory,** because glory sometimes follows those who seek to avoid it, and if they are obliged to receive it, they should not love it. Furthermore, [spirit] connotes vehemence: "Who can bear the violence of one provoked?" (Prov. 27:4). It also connotes wrath. And as to this he says, **provoking one another,** namely, to quarrels and fights or other unlawful things: "Not in contention and envy" (Rom. 13:13). Furthermore, it is a spirit of sadness, of which it is said in Proverbs (17:22): "A sorrowful spirit drieth up the bones." And concerning this he says, **envying one another:** "Envy is the rottenness of the bones," because it alone feeds on the good (Prov. 14:30).

# CHAPTER 6

## LECTURE 1

1 Brethren, and if a man be overtaken in any fault, you, who are spiritual, instruct such a one in the spirit of meekness, considering thyself, lest thou also be tempted.

2 Bear ye one another's burdens; and so you shall fulfil the law of Christ.

3 For if any man think himself to be something, whereas he is nothing, he deceiveth himself.

4 But let every one prove his own work; and so he shall have glory in himself only and not in another.

5 For every one shall bear his own burden.

After leading the Galatians back to the state of truth as to divine things, the Apostle then leads them back as to things human, instructing them how to behave toward men.

First, how to act toward the upright;
Secondly, toward those who are wicked (v. 11).

With respect to the first, he does three things:

First, he teaches how superiors should act toward inferiors;
Secondly, how equals toward equals (v. 2);
Thirdly, how inferiors toward superiors (v. 6).

Regarding the first he does two things:

First, he sets forth the admonition;
Secondly, he assigns the reason for the admonition (v. 1): **considering thyself, lest thou also be tempted.**

Therefore, because he had said so much about sin, then, lest anyone free of sin be severe toward sinners, he gives

them an admonition about meekness and mercy, saying:
**Brethren, and if a man be overtaken in any fault, you, who
are spiritual, instruct such a one in the spirit of meekness.**
Herein he lays down the three elements which form the
admonition. The first consists in being come upon unawares.
For when some sin out of malice, they are less worthy of
forgiveness: "Who as it were on purpose have revolted from
him and would not understand all his ways" (Job 34:27).
But when one is overtaken by temptation and lured into sin,
pardon should be granted him more readily. That is why he
says, **and if a man be overtaken in any fault,** i.e., fall through
want of circumspection and because of trickery, so that he
could not escape, **instruct such a one in the spirit of meekness.** The second is infrequency of sin. For some sin as a
matter of custom: "Cursing and lying and killing and theft
and adultery have overflowed and blood hath touched blood"
(Os. 4:2). Against such sinners more severe measures should
be taken. And this is excluded when he says, **in any,** imply-
ing that he is speaking of those who do not sin as a daily
practice. The third is the quality of the sin. For some sins
consist in commission and some in omission. And the first is
more grave than the second, because the former are opposed
to negative precepts which bind always and at every moment;
whereas the latter, being opposed to affirmative precepts,
since they do not bind one at every moment, it cannot be
known definitely when they do bind. Hence it is said in
Psalm 18 (13): "Who can understand sins?" And touching
this he says, **in any fault.** Or, according to a Gloss, a fault
is a sin committed through ignorance.

Having stated these things, he recommends that mercy
be shown by those who correct others. These are spiritual
men whose office is to correct. Hence he says, **those who
are spiritual, instruct such a one in the spirit of meekness:**
"The spiritual man judgeth all things, and he himself is
judged of no man" (1 Cor. 2:15). The reason for this is that
he has a correct judgment of all things, being rightly dis-

posed to each thing, as a person with a healthy taste is the
best judge of flavor. Now the spiritual man alone is rightly
disposed concerning moral actions. Therefore he alone judges
well of them.

But although the name "spirit" suggests unyielding en-
ergy, according to the saying of Isaias (25:4): "For the spirit
of the mighty is like a whirlwind beating against a wall,"
it should not be supposed that spiritual men are over-strict
in correcting. For the spirit of this world does that, but the
Holy Spirit produces a certain gentleness and sweetness in a
man: "O, how good and sweet is thy spirit, O Lord, in all
things" (Wis. 12:1). Hence he says, **in the spirit of meekness:** "The just man shall correct me in mercy and shall reprove me" (Ps. 140:5). Contrariwise, it is said of some in
Ezechiel (34:4): "You ruled over them with vigor and with
a high hand." Furthermore, he says, **instruct,** and not "correct," because he is speaking of those who fall by being overtaken, and these need instruction; or because every sinner
falls through some lack of knowledge: "They err that work
evil" (Prov. 14:22).

He adds a reason for the admonition, saying, **considering thyself, lest thou also be tempted.** As if to say: You
should do as I say, because you, too, are weak. For as long
as we are in this mortal life, we are prone to sin. But nothing so breaks a man from severity in correcting as fear of
his own fall: "Judge of the disposition of thy neighbor by
thyself" (Ecclus. 31:18).

But how they ought to act towards equals he shows when
he says, **Bear ye one another's burdens.**

First, he sets down the admonition;
Secondly, he assigns a reason for it (v. 2);
Thirdly, he removes an obstacle to the admonition (v.
3).

Here he admonishes them to support one another, saying, **Bear ye one another's burdens.** And this is to be done

in three ways. In one way by patiently enduring the bodily
or spiritual defects of another: "We that are stronger ought
to bear the infirmities of the weak" (Rom. 15:1). In a second way by coming to one another's aid in their needs:
"Communicating to the necessities of the saints" (Rom. 12:13).
In a third way by making satisfaction through prayers and
works for the punishment one has incurred: "A brother that
is helped by his brother is like a strong city" (Prov. 18:19).
Now the reason for this admonition is the fulfillment of the
law of Christ. But this is charity: "The fulfillment of the
law is love" (Rom. 13:10). Hence he says: **and you shall
fulfil the law of Christ,** i.e., charity.

There are three reasons why charity is specifically linked
with the law of Christ. First, because by it the New Law is
distinguished from the Old; for the former is a law of fear,
but the latter of love. Hence Augustine says: "Fear and love
is the slight difference between the Old Law and the New."
Secondly, because Christ expressly promulgated His law in
terms of charity: "By this shall all men know that you are
my disciples, if you have love one for another" (Jn. 13:35);
again: "A new commandment I give unto you: that you love
one another, as I have loved you" (v. 34). Thirdly, because
Christ fulfilled it and left us an example how to fulfill it;
for he bore our sins out of charity: "Surely he hath borne
our infirmities" (Is. 53:4); "Who his own self bore our sins
in his body upon the tree, that we, being dead to sins, should
live to justice" (1 Pet. 2:24); "He himself shall carry them
that are with young" (Is. 40:11). Thus, then, ought we to
carry one another's burdens out of charity, that so we may
fulfill the law of Christ.

The obstacle to fulfilling the above admonition is pride.
And to exclude this he says, **For if any man think himself
to be something, whereas he is nothing, he deceiveth himself.**

First, he censures such pride;
Secondly, he points out how to avoid it (v. 4);
Thirdly, he gives a reason for avoiding it (v. 5).

He says therefore: Do as I say. But it sometimes happens that one does not carry another's burdens, because he prefers himself to others. Hence such a one said in Luke (18:11): "I am not as the rest of men, extortioners, unjust, adulterers." Therefore he says, **For if any man think himself to be something,** i.e., through pride judge in his own mind that he is greater in comparison to a sinner, **whereas he is nothing** of himself, because whatever we are is from the grace of God, according to the saying of the Apostle: "But by the grace of God I am what I am" (1 Cor. 15:10), anyone, I say, who acts thus **deceiveth himself,** i.e., cuts himself off from the truth: "All nations are before him as if they had no being at all" (Is. 40:17); "When you have done all these things that are commanded you, say: We are unprofitable servants: we have done that which we ought to do" (Lk. 17:10).

Now the way to avoid such a failing is to consider one's own defects, for it is because one considers the defects of others and not his own that he seems to himself to be something in comparison to others in whom he observes defects; and not considering his own, he has a feeling of pride. Hence he says, **But let every one prove,** i.e., diligently examine, **his,** i.e., his own, **work,** both inward and outward: "Let a man prove himself" (1 Cor. 11:28), **and so in himself,** i.e., in his own conscience, **he shall have glory,** i.e., shall glory and rejoice—"For our glory is this, the testimony of our conscience" (2 Cor. 1:12)—**and not in another,** i.e., not in being praised by someone else. Or thus: **in himself,** i.e., in things that are his own, **he will have glory,** i.e., he will glory by considering himself; **and not in another,** i.e., not by considering others: "Gladly, therefore, will I glory in my infirmities, that the power of Christ may dwell in me" (2 Cor. 12:9). Or, **in himself,** i.e., in God Who dwells in him, **he will glory,** i.e., the glory will be His; **and not in any other** save in God: "He that glorieth, let him glory in the Lord" (2 Cor. 10:17).

The reason for avoiding pride is the reward or punishment that will be rendered to each one according to his merits or demerits. Hence he says, **For every one shall bear his own burden.** But this seems contrary to what he had said earlier, namely, **Bear ye one another's burdens.**

But it should be known that he was speaking there of the burden of supporting weakness, a burden which we ought to carry one for another; but now he is speaking of the burden of rendering an account. This, everyone will carry for himself, whether it be a burden of reward or of punishment. For "burden" signifies the weight sometimes of punishment, sometimes of reward: "Working for us an eternal weight of glory" (2 Cor. 4:17); "Say to the just man that it is well, for he shall eat the fruit of his doings. Woe to the wicked unto evil: for the reward of his hands shall be given him" (Is. 3:10). But if some are said to render an account for others, as prelates for subjects, according to Ezechiel (3:20): "I will require his blood at thy hand"; and Hebrews (13:17): "Obey your prelates . . . , for they watch as being to render an account of your souls"; this is not contrary to the words of the Apostle, because they are not punished for the sins of their subjects but for their own, which they committed in ruling them.

Therefore pride and sin are to be avoided, because everyone will present to God on the day of judgment his own burden, i.e., the measure of his own grace as sheaves of good works: "But coming they shall come with joyfulness, carrying their sheaves," and this refers to those who are good (Ps. 125:7). Or: **will carry his own burden,** i.e., each the punishment for his own sin.

# CHAPTER 6

## LECTURE 2

6 And let him that is instructed in the word, communicate to
him, that instructeth him, in all good things.

7 Be not deceived; God is not mocked.

8 For what things a man shall sow, those also shall he reap. For
he that soweth in his flesh of the flesh also shall reap corruption. But
he that soweth in the spirit of the spirit shall reap life everlasting.

9 And in doing good, let us not fail; for in due time we shall
reap, not failing.

10 Therefore, whilst we have time, let us work good to all men,
but especially to those who are of the household of the faith.

After showing how those who are greater should act toward those below them, and how equals should act toward
equals, the Apostle then shows here how those who are lesser
should serve and revere those who are over them. About this
he does three things:

First, he advises that they serve readily;
Secondly, that they serve perseveringly (v. 9);
Thirdly, that they serve all (v. 10).

Regarding the first he does two things:

First, he lays down the admonition to serve;
Secondly, he forestalls an excuse (v. 7).

He says therefore: We have indicated above how those
who are greater should act toward those who are below them,
namely, by correcting them in a gentle manner and by instructing. Now, however, there remains to see how the lesser
should accommodate themselves to those who are higher.
Therefore he says, **Let him that is instructed in the word,**
i.e., taught the word of God, **communicate to him that in-**

**structeth him,** i.e., who teaches him; let him, I say, communicate to him **in all good things.**

But it should be noted that a disciple can communicate in two ways with his teacher. First, so as to receive good things from the teacher; and so it is said, **Let him that is instructed in the word communicate,** i.e., make common to himself what belonged to the teacher, by imitating him: "Be imitators of me, as I also am of Christ" (1 Cor. 11:1). But because teachers might at times not do what is good, they are not to be imitated in this. Hence he adds, **in all good things:** "Whatsoever they shall say to you, observe and do: but according to their works, do ye not" (Mt. 23:3). Secondly, that he communicate his own goods to the teacher. For this is commanded by the Lord: "They who preach the gospel should live by the gospel" (1 Cor. 9:14); "The workman is worthy of his meat" (Mt. 10:10); "The laborer is worthy of his hire" (Lk. 10:7); and the Apostle says, "If we have sown unto you spiritual things, is it a great matter if we reap your carnal things?" (1 Cor. 9:11). And therefore he says here, **Let him that is instructed in the word communicate to him that instructeth,** i.e., the one taught should communicate to the teacher, **in all good things** that he has; for even temporal things are called goods: "If you be willing and will hearken to me, you shall eat the good things of the land" (Is. 1:19); "If you then, being evil, know how to give good gifts to your children: how much more will your Father who is in heaven give good things to them that ask him?" (Mt. 7:11).

But he says, **in all good things,** because one should not communicate solely to those who are in dire need; but whatever one has he ought universally to communicate to his neighbor, including knowledge and advice and influence: "As every man hath received grace, administering the same one to another" (1 Pet. 4:10). Of this sharing it is said in Romans (12:13): "Communicating to the necessities of the saints"; "In dividing by lot give and take" (Ecclus. 14:15).

Then when he says, **Be not deceived; God is not mocked,**
he forestalls an excuse.

First, he forestalls it;
Secondly, he gives a reason for this (v. 8).

He says, therefore: **Be not deceived; God is not mocked.**
This can be taken in two ways, according to the two explanations given above. According to the first, this way: You
say that we ought to imitate our teachers even in good
things, but I cannot imitate them save in the things they
do; and the only thing I observe in them is evil. Therefore,
I ought to imitate them in evil. But he dismisses this, when
he says, **Be not deceived, God is not mocked.** As if to say:
It is erroneous to say this, for the evils of the prelates do not
excuse us, because they are an example to their subjects only
in those matters in which they imitate Christ, Who is the
shepherd without sin. Hence he expressly says in John
(10:11): "I am the good shepherd"; and the Apostle says in
1 Corinthians (4:16); (11:1): "Be imitators of me, as I also
am of Christ." As if to say: Imitate me in those things in
which I imitate Christ. And although you excuse yourself
before men because of the evil acts of prelates, yet **God is
not mocked,** i.e., cannot be deceived: "Shall he be deceived
as a man, with your deceitful dealings?" (Job 13:9). Hence
it is said in Proverbs (3:34): "He shall scorn the scorners."

But according to the second explanation it is understood
in the following manner. They could say: We are poor and
have nothing to communicate. But he rejects this, saying, **Be
not deceived,** i.e., think not to excuse yourself in vain, by
pretending poverty; **God is not mocked,** i.e., cannot be deceived, for He knows our hearts and is not unaware of our
possessions. A likely excuse may deceive a man and satisfy
him; but it cannot deceive God.

He assigns the reason for this, saying, **For what things
a man shall sow, those also shall he reap.**

First, in a general way;
Secondly, in a specific way (v. 8).

He says therefore with respect to the first explanation: Surely you err in believing this, because God will render to each one according to his own merits: **For what things a man shall sow, those also shall he reap,** i.e., he will be rewarded or punished according to his works, be they good or evil, great or small. But according to the second explanation: **what things a man shall sow, those also shall he reap;** i.e., he will be rewarded according to his good deeds, great or small, both as to the quality of the works and the quantity of the good deeds: "He that soweth sparingly, shall also reap sparingly; and he who soweth in blessings, shall also reap blessings" (2 Cor. 9:6).

Then he assigns a specific reason, saying, **For he that soweth in his flesh, of the flesh also shall reap corruption.** Now this reason has two parts, according to the two sowings: namely, in the flesh and in the spirit.

First therefore, he treats of the sowing in the flesh, where we must first of all see what it is to sow in the flesh;
Secondly, what it is, "of the flesh to reap corruption."

To sow in the flesh is to work for the body and for the flesh. As though I were to say: I have spent much on that man, i.e., I have done many things for him. Hence he sows in the flesh who in all that he does, even in things that seem good, does them to favor and benefit the flesh. But with respect to reaping corruption of the flesh, he says and infers, that because seed fructifies for the most part according to the condition of the land, we see that on some lands wheat seeds degenerate into siligo or something else. Now the condition of the flesh is that it is corruptible; hence **he that soweth in his flesh,** i.e., directs his works and interest to the flesh, must expect that those works corrupt and perish: "Every work that is corruptible shall fail in the end" (Ecclus. 14:20); "For if you live according to the flesh, you shall die" (Rom. 8:13).

Secondly, he treats of the sowing in the spirit, saying, **But he that soweth in the spirit,** i.e., directs his interest to the service of the spirit by serving justice through faith and charity, **shall reap** from the spirit according to its condition. Now the condition of the spirit is that it is the principle of life: "It is the spirit that giveth life," and not just any life, but eternal life; since the spirit is immortal (Jn. 6:64). Hence, **of the spirit he shall reap life everlasting:** "To him that soweth justice there is a faithful reward," because it never withers (Prov. 11:18).

But note that when he treats of the sowing in the flesh, he says, **in his flesh,** because the flesh is ours, as part of our nature; but when he speaks of the seed of the spirit, he does not say "his own," because the spirit in us is not from ourselves but from God.

Then when he says, **And in doing good, let us not fail,** he counsels perseverance in ministering, because we should do good not only for a time but always. This can be referred to those already mentioned, namely, to superiors, to equals, and to those who are lower. As if to say: Whatever our station, whether prelates towards subjects, or equals toward equals, or subjects toward prelates, **in doing good, let us not fail,** i.e., in doing good works; because in reaping we shall not fail: "Whatsoever thy hand is able to do, do it earnestly" (Ecclus. 9:10); "Be ye steadfast and unmovable" (1 Cor. 15:58). And it is important that we do not fail; because we hope for an eternal and unfailing reward. Hence he adds: **for in due time we shall reap, not failing.** Therefore Augustine says: "If a man puts no limit on his works, God will put none on His reward." But note that he says, **in due time:** because a farmer does not immediately reap the fruit of what he sows, but at the suitable time: "Behold the husbandman waits for the precious fruit of the earth; patiently bearing till he receive the early and latter rain" (Jas.

5:7). Of this harvest it is said: "Who soweth in blessings shall also reap of the blessings, eternal life" (2 Cor. 9:6).

Then when he says, **Whilst we have time, let us work good to all men,** he advises everyone to minister, saying: Since we shall reap, not failing, then **whilst we have time,** i.e., in this life, which is the time for sowing: "I must work the works of him that sent me, whilst it is day: the night cometh, when no man can work" (Jn. 9:4); "Whatsoever thy hand is able to do, do it earnestly; for neither work nor reason nor wisdom nor knowledge shall be in hell whither thou art hastening" (Ecclus. 9:10). As long, I say, as we have time, **let us work good,** and this to all men who are bound to us through a divine likeness, inasmuch as all of us have been made to the image of God.

But this seems to be contrary to Ecclesiasticus (12:5): "Give to the good and receive not the sinner." Therefore we are not obliged to do good to everyone. I answer that in the sinner are two things: namely, his nature and his guilt. Now the nature in everyone, including an enemy, must be loved and upheld: "Love your enemies" (Mt. 5:44). But the guilt in them is to be shunned. Therefore, when it is said, "Give to the just and receive not the sinner," the meaning is that you ought not to do good to the sinner precisely as he is a sinner, but because he is a human being. Hence Augustine says: "Be not remiss in judging, or inhuman in helping. Therefore, in evil men let us attack their sin, but show mercy to our common condition."

But because we cannot do good to everyone, he presents the order in which it is to be done, when he adds: **but especially to those who are of the household of the faith,** who, namely, are not only akin to us in nature but united by faith and grace: "You are no more strangers and foreigners: but you are fellow citizens of the saints and the domestics of God" (Eph. 2:19). Therefore mercy must be extended to everyone but preferably to the just who share in the faith, because it is said: "But if any man have not care of his own and especially those of his house, he hath denied the faith and is worse than an infidel" (1 Tim. 5:8).

But here it might be asked whether it is lawful to love one more than another. To answer this, it should be noted that love can be called greater or less in two ways. In one way, from the standpoint of the object; in another, from the intensity of the act. For to love someone is to will good to him. Accordingly, one can love one person more than another, either because he wills him a greater good, which is the object of love, or because he more intensely wills him a good, i.e., with a more intense love. Therefore, with respect to the first, we ought to love everyone equally, because we ought to wish the good of eternal life to everyone; but with respect to the second, it is not necessary that we love all equally, because since the intensity of an act results from the principle of the action, and the principle of the action is union and similarity, we ought to love in a higher degree and more intensely those who are more like us and more closely united to us.

# CHAPTER 6

## LECTURE 3

11 See what a letter I have written to you with my own hand.
12 For as many as desire to please in the flesh, they constrain you to be circumcised, only that they may not suffer the persecution of the cross of Christ.
13 For neither they themselves who are circumcised keep the law; but they will have you to be circumcised, that they may glory in your flesh.

After admonishing the Galatians how to behave towards men who are upright and just, the Apostle here teaches them how to act toward heretics and the perverse.

First, he insinuates the way he is writing the admonition;

Secondly, he sets forth the admonition (v. 12).

As to the first, it should be noted that heretics were wont to distort and falsify the canonical scriptures and append things that savored of heresy. Because of this, whenever the Apostle wrote anything against them, he followed the practice of writing something at the end of the epistle, so that it could not be distorted. In this way it could be known that it came from him with full knowledge of its contents. Thus in 1 Corinthians (16:21) he says: "The salutation of me, Paul, with my own hand." For he allowed the entire epistle to be written by someone else at his dictation; then, at the end, he added something in his own hand. According to this procedure, then, whatever followed from that place on, Paul wrote in his own hand. Hence he says; **See what a letter I have written to you with my own hand;** to the end, namely, that you might firmly hold to the foregoing, and that knowing this epistle is sent by me, you might obey better. In this way, then, prelates ought to write in their own hand, so that what they teach by word and script, they may show by example. Hence it is said in Isaias (49:16): "I have graven thee in my hands" (i.e., works); and in Exodus (Ch. 32) it is said of Moses that he descended carrying two stone tablets written by the finger of God.

He then follows with the admonition, saying, **For as many as desire to please in the flesh, they constrain you to be circumcised.**

First, he exposes the intention of the seducers;

Secondly, he shows that his intention is contrary to theirs (v. 14).

Regarding the first, he does two things:

First, he discloses the evil intention of the seducers;

Secondly, he proves what he says (v. 13).

Concerning the first, he lays down one fact and two intentions that are mutually related. The fact concerns those who urged circumcision, from which they intended two things, one for the sake of the other; namely, that they might thereby please the Jews for having introduced the observances of the Law in the Church of the Gentiles. And this is what he says: **As many as desire to please,** namely, the unbelieving Jews, **they constrain you to be circumcised** not by absolute force, but, as it were, by placing a condition, saying: "Except you be circumcised after the manner of Moses, you cannot be saved," as is recorded in Acts (15:1).

They further intended to derive some security from this. For the Jews persecuted the disciples of Christ, because of the preaching of the Cross: "But we preach Christ crucified, unto the Jews, indeed, a stumbling-block, and unto the Gentiles, foolishness" (1 Cor. 1:23). And this because through the preaching of the Cross the works of the Law were made void. For if the apostles had preached, along with the Cross of Christ, that the legal ceremonies were to be observed, the Jews would not have persecuted the apostles. Hence he said: **And I, brethren, if I yet preach circumcision, why do I yet suffer persecution?** (5:11). Therefore, in order to escape persecution from the Jews, some urged circumcision. So he says: And they do this for the **only** reason **that they may not suffer the persecution of the cross of Christ,** a persecution which is launched because of the Cross of Christ.

Or they did this to escape the persecution not only of the Jews but of the Gentile unbelievers. For the Roman Emperors, Cajus Caesar and Octavius Augustus, promulgated laws that wherever there were Jews, they might observe their own rite and ceremonies. Consequently, anyone who believed in Christ and was not circumcised was subject to persecution from the Gentiles and Jews. Therefore, in order that they might not be troubled because of their faith in Christ and that they might live in peace, they constrained them to be circumcised, as is mentioned in a Gloss.

But because the false brethren might say that they urged circumcision not for that reason, but solely because of their zeal for the Law, then excluding this, he proves his proposition thus, when he says: **For neither they themselves who are circumcised keep the law.** For it is obvious that if through zeal for the Law they urged certain ones to observe the Law, they should also command the Law to be fulfilled in other matters. But neither those who are circumcised nor the false brethren keep the Law in other matters, namely, in moral matters, which are more important in the Law, and in other observances: "None of you keeps the law" (Jn. 7:19). Therefore it was not from zeal for the Law that they urged circumcision: "Circumcision profiteth, indeed, if you keep the law" (Rom. 2:25). **But** the reason why **they will have you to be circumcised** is **that in your flesh,** i.e., in your fleshly circumcision, **they may glory** among the Jews for making so many proselytes; "Woe to you, scribes and Pharisees, hypocrites; because you go round about the sea and the land to make one proselyte; and when he is made, you make him the child of hell twofold more than yourselves" (Mt. 23:15).

# CHAPTER 6

## LECTURE 4

14 But God forbid that I should glory, save in the cross of our Lord Jesus Christ; by whom the world is crucified to me, and I to the world.

15 For in Christ Jesus neither circumcision availeth any thing, nor uncircumcision; but a new creature.

After unmasking the sinister intention of the seducers, the Apostle here insinuates his own intention.

First, he states his intention;
Secondly, he gives a sign of this intention (v. 14);
Thirdly, the reason for this intention (v. 15).

He says therefore: The intention of the seducers is obvious, for they glory in the flesh; but I seek my glory elsewhere, namely, in the Cross. And this is what he says: **But God forbid that I should glory, save in the cross of our Lord Jesus Christ.** Notice that where the worldly philosopher felt shame, there the Apostle found his treasure: what the former regarded as foolish became for the Apostle wisdom and glory, as Augustine says. For each person glories in that through which he is considered great. Thus a person who regards himself as great in his riches, glories in them; and so on for other things. For one who regards himself to be great in nothing but Christ glories in Christ alone. But the Apostle was such a one; hence he says: **I live now not I; but Christ liveth in me** (2:20).

Accordingly he glories in nothing but Christ and particularly in the Cross of Christ; and this because in it are found all the things about which men usually glory. For some glory in the friendship of the great, such as of kings and princes; and this friendship the Apostle found most of all in the Cross, because there an obvious sign of divine friendship is shown: "But God commendeth his charity towards us; because when as yet we were sinners according to the time, Christ died for us" (Rom. 5:8). For nothing shows His mercy to us as much as the death of Christ. Hence Gregory: "O inestimable love of charity! To redeem the servant, He delivered His Son."

Again, some glory in knowledge; and of this the Apostle found a more excellent one in the Cross: "For I judged not myself to know anything among you but Jesus Christ and him crucified" (1 Cor. 2:2). For in the Cross is the perfection of all law and the whole art of living well. Again, some glory in power; and of this the Apostle found the highest form through the Cross: "The word of the cross to them, indeed, that perish is foolishness; but to them that are saved, that is, to us, it is the power of God." (1 Cor. 1:18). Again, some glory in newly-found freedom; and this the Apostle obtained through the Cross: "Our old man is crucified with him that the body of sin may be destroyed, to the end that we may serve sin no longer" (Rom. 6:6).

Again, some glory in being accepted into some famous fellowship; but by the Cross of Christ, we are accepted into the heavenly ranks: "Making peace through the blood of his cross, both as to the things that are on earth and the things that are in heaven" (Col. 1:20). Again, some glory in the triumphal banners of conquest; but the Cross is the triumphal ensign of Christ's conquest over the demons: "And despoiling the principalities and powers, he hath exposed them confidently in open show, triumphing over them in himself" (Col. 2:15); "Blessed is the wood by which justice cometh" (Wis. 14:7).

The sign of his own intention he shows, saying **by whom the world is crucified to me, and I to the world.** But since this which he says, **But God forbid that I should glory save in the cross of our Lord Jesus Christ,** is an exceptive proposition which includes one affirmative and one negative statement, he is really giving two signs that prove both statements. First, he proves the negative one, namely, that he does not glory save in the cross. He does this when he says, **by whom the world is crucified to me, and I to the world.** For that in which a person glories is not dead in his heart, but rather that which he scorns: "I am forgotten as one dead, from the heart" (Ps. 30:13). But it is plain that the world and all things in it were dead in the heart of Paul: "I count all things as dung, that I may gain Christ" (Phil. 3:8). Therefore he does not glory in the world or in the things that are in the world. And this is what he says: Verily, **I glory in nothing save in the cross of Christ, by whom,** namely, Christ crucified, **the world is crucified to me,** i.e., is dead in my heart, so that I covet nothing in it.

Secondly, he proves the affirmative, namely, that he

glories in the Cross of Christ, saying that he is crucified to the World. For a person who glories in something treasures it and desires to make it known; but the Apostle treasures nothing or desires to make nothing known except what pertains to the Cross of Christ; therefore, he glories in it alone. And this is what he says: **and I to the world,** namely, I am crucified. As if to say: I carry the marks of the Cross and I am considered as dead. Therefore, as the world abhors the Cross of Christ, so it abhors me: "For you are dead and your life is hid with Christ in God" (Col. 3:3).

The reason why he glories in nothing else is given when he says, **For in Christ Jesus neither circumcision availeth any thing nor uncircumcision, but a new creature.** Indeed, he glories mainly in that which avails and helps in joining him to Christ; for it is this the Apostle desires, namely, to be with Christ. And because the Jewish rite and the observances of the Gentiles are of no avail in this regard, but only the Cross of Christ, therefore he glories in it alone. And this is what he says: **For in Christ Jesus neither circumcision,** i.e., the Jewish rite, **nor uncircumcision,** i.e., Gentile observances, **availeth any thing,** i.e., to justify us and join us to Christ, **but a new creature** availeth for us. This, indeed, is obvious from what was said above, in almost the same words: **For in Christ Jesus neither circumcision availeth anything nor uncircumcision; but faith that worketh by charity** (5:6). Therefore, faith informed by charity is the new creature. For we have been created and made to exist in our nature through Adam, but that creature is already old. Therefore, the Lord in producing us and establishing us in the existence of grace has made a new creature: "That we might be some beginning of his creature" (Jas. 1:18). And it is called "new," because by it we are reborn into a new life by the Holy Spirit— "Thou shalt send forth thy spirit and they shall be created: and thou shalt renew the face of the earth" (Ps. 103:30)— and by the Cross of Christ: "If then any be in Christ a new creature, the old things are passed away, behold all things are made new" (2 Cor. 5:17). In this way, then, by a new creature, i.e., by the faith of Christ and the charity of God which has been poured out in our hearts, we are made new and are joined to Christ.

# CHAPTER 6

## LECTURE 5

16 And whosoever shall follow this rule, peace on them and mercy; and upon the Israel of God.
17 From henceforth let no man be troublesome to me; for I bear the marks of the Lord Jesus in my body.
18 The grace of our Lord Jesus Christ be with your spirit, brethren. Amen.

Having disclosed the intention of the seducers and intimated his own, the Apostle counsels them:

First, to imitate him;
Secondly, to desist from being troublesome to him (v. 17);
Thirdly, he begs grace for them to carry out the aforesaid (v. 18).

First, therefore, he says: My intention is to glory only in the Cross of Christ. And you, too, should do this, because **whosoever shall follow this rule** which I follow, namely, this proper way of glorying—"But we will not glory beyond our measure and according to the measure of the rule which God hath measured to us" (2 Cor. 10:13)—**peace on them**, namely, on those who glory, because they glory in Christ alone: peace, I say, by which they are set at rest and made perfect in good. (For peace is tranquillity of mind: "Since I am become in his presence as one finding peace" (Cant. 8:10); and in Colossians (3:15): "And let the peace of Christ rejoice in your hearts, wherein also you are called in one body"): **and mercy,** by which we are set free of our sins: "The mercies of the Lord that we are not consumed" (Lam. 3:22); "The grace of God and his mercy is with his saints, and he hath respect to his chosen," namely, who are His Israel (Wis. 4:15): "For it is not he is a Jew who is so outwardly" (Rom. 2:28). He, therefore, is **the Israel of God** who is spiritually an Israel before God: "Behold an Israelite indeed, in whom there is no guile" (Jn. 1:47); "For all are not Israelites that are of Israel: neither are all they that are the seed of Abraham, children; but in Isaac shall thy seed be called; that is to say, not they that are the children of the flesh are the children of God but they that are the children of the promise, are accounted for the seed" (Rom. 9:6). Hence even the Gentiles have become the Israel of God by uprightness of mind; for Israel means "most upright": "Israel will be your name" (Gen. 32:28).

Then when he says, **From henceforth let no man be troublesome to me,** he admonishes them to bother him no more.

First, he gives the admonition;
Secondly, he gives a reason for it (v. 17).

He says therefore: **From henceforth let no man be troublesome to me.** This can be explained in two ways. In one way, **from henceforth** can be taken as one word [*amodo*], so that the sense is: **From henceforth,** i.e., from now on. In another way it might be taken as two words [*de cetero*], so that the sense is: Let no man be troublesome to me about anything else. As if to say: I glory in the Cross alone; with respect to anything else, let no man bother me, because I care about nothing else. But the first is better.

His saying, **let no man be troublesome to me,** can be referred to the false brethren, who were troubling the Apos-

tle by raising difficulties and murmuring about the legal observances: "But as for me, when they were troublesome, I
was clothed with haircloth" (Ps. 34:13). Or it can be referred
to hearers who do not grasp his meaning. As if to say: **let
no one be troublesome to me**, i.e., let no one who hears me
show himself to be such as to make it necessary for me to
labor with him again, namely, by understanding in a way
other than I have taught.

The reason for this admonition he assigns when he says,
**for I bear the marks [stigmata] of the Lord Jesus in my body.**
For stigmata are, strictly speaking, certain marks branded
on one with a hot iron; as when a slave is marked on the
face by his master, so that no one else will claim him, but
quietly let him remain with the master whose marks he bears.
And this is the way the Apostle says he bears the marks of
the Lord, branded, as it were, as a slave of Christ; and this,
because he bore the marks of Christ's passion, suffering many
tribulations in his body for Him, according to the saying of
1 Peter (2:21): "Christ suffered for us, leaving you an example, that you should follow his steps"; "Always bearing
about in our body the mortification of Jesus, that the life
also of Jesus may be made manifest in our mortal flesh"
(2 Cor. 4:10).

According to this there are two ways of connecting this
with the preceding. In one way, as has been said: **let no
man be troublesome to me**, for I bear the marks of Our
Lord Jesus Christ in my body; consequently, no one has
any right over me except Christ. In another way: **let no man
be troublesome to me**, because I have many other conflicts
and marks that trouble me in the persecutions I suffer; and
it is cruel to add affliction to one already afflicted. Hence the
complaint of Job (16:15): "He hath torn me with wound
upon wound." Nevertheless, the first is better.

Then he implores the help of God's grace, saying: **The
grace of our Lord Jesus Christ**, by which you may carry out
the foregoing, **be with your spirit**, i.e., with your understand-

ing, so that you may understand the truth. Or, **with your spirit,** with which you should observe the Law, rather than in a carnal manner: "For you have not received the spirit of bondage again in fear; but you have received the spirit of adoption of sons" (Rom. 8:15).

# Index of Names

Alexander, 51
Alexander the Great, 7
Ambrose, St., 38, 51, 69
Aristotle, 67, 96, 179
Augustine, St., 49–52, 58, 66, 68, 69, 73, 95, 118, 151–53, 160, 161, 166, 169, 173, 190, 198, 203
Avicenna, 67, 68

Brennus, 7

Cajus Caesar, 201
Claudius, 34
Cyprian, 51

Didymus, 51
Dionysius, 138

Ebion, 115
Elvidius, 28

Jerome, St., 29, 49–51, 57, 68, 151, 172
John Chrysostom, 37
Julian, 160

Laudicens, 51
Leo, Pope, 49

Nestorius, 115

Octavius Augustus, 201
Origen, 51

The Philosopher, see Aristotle
Photinus, 114
Porphyry, 160